MW00577305

Creating Transformational Churches

A Guide to Reignite Your Church's Growth

By

Thomas Manning

Foreword by
Alton Garrison

CREATING TRANSFORMATIONAL CHURCHES: *A GUIDE TO REIGNITE YOUR CHURCH'S GROWTH*

Amazon Publishing Agency
870 N Main St, Sheridan, WY 82801, United States

ISBN 13: 978-1-916761-27-8

Cataloguing-in-Publication Data

Creating Transformational Churches: A Guide to Reignite Your Church's Growth by Thomas Manning; foreword by Alton Garrison.

iv + 114 p.; 23 cm. Includes bibliographical references.
ISBN 13: 978-1-916761-27-8
I. Manning, Thomas. II. Garrison, Alton.
III. Creating Transformational Churches: A Guide to the Transformational Process of Church Growth.

Manufactured in the U.S.A.   2023

Cover Design: Steven DaSilva

Table of Contents

Dedication i

Acknowledgments.. ii

About the Author iv

Foreword vi

Preface ix

Introduction..1

Chapter 1 The State of the Church....................................3

Chapter 2 Major Causes for Plateau and Decline 10

Chapter 3 The Process of Transformation 16

Chapter 4 Creating New Lifecycles 41

Chapter 5 Creating a New Lifecycle in CLC 53

Chapter 6 The Process of Making Disciples...................71

Chapter 7 Making Disciples: SHARE 81

Chapter 8 Making Disciples: CONNECT.......................88

Chapter 9 Making Disciples: TRAIN 93

Chapter 10 Making Disciples: RELEASE 98

Conclusion 104

"Tom hits the nail on the head regarding the challenges of today's church, and they should not be ignored. The process of church revitalization begins with the transformation of the leader. Many leaders desire to change but often struggle in the actualization of it. The 'Divine Urgencies' shared in this book are great tools to begin revitalizing churches that have stagnated. This book provides more than handles, though; it also serves as a mirror for leaders for a real evaluation of where they are and where their ministries are at."

— Rev Dominic Yeo
Secretary, World Assemblies of God Fellowship
Chairman, Asia Pacific Assemblies of God
General Superintendent, The Assemblies of God of Singapore
Lead Pastor, Trinity Christian Centre, Singapore

"I recommend *Creating Transformational Churches* to church leaders and anyone passionate about church health. Tom Manning addresses a topic that flies under the radar of the oft-addressed paradigm of 'successful, growing churches,' and that is churches in decline. Starting fresh with a church plant is one thing; guiding a church from decline to growth is another. The Manning's are long-time associates and friends from serving together in Europe, so I know Tom speaks from experience. This book offers both a biblical foundation of discipleship and practical tools to address present-day reality. It will help those who care deeply about leading a local body of Christ back to a place of thriving community and ministry."

—Dr. Greg Mundis
Assemblies of God World Missions Executive Director

"We know that plateaued ministries quickly become dying institutions if they are not guided by turnaround leaders. In this book, Pastor Tom Manning shares the crucial principles necessary to jumpstart new waves of church growth. For anyone facing a church in plateau or decline, this is a must-read book."

—Dr. Kent J. Ingle
President, Southeastern University

"I am excited to recommend *Creating Transformational Churches: A Guide to Reignite Your Churches Growth.* Thomas Manning firmly confronts a dangerous trend in the contemporary American Church: decline. However, unlike most current critics, he does not simply lament the problem and walk away. He offers genuine and trustable solutions. Transformation in plateaued or declining churches is a process, not an event, he says. A process for creating a new and positive lifestyle will bring a lasting victory. Manning instructs leaders to share the good news with those who need it most, connect converts to the congregation, train them to be effective disciples, and release them to expand the kingdom of God. This process will enlarge the church and advance the Kingdom. This book will help and guide any pastor who takes it seriously and applies its instructions. Transformation. Read it. Do it."

—Dr. Terry Rayburn
Superintendent, Peninsular Florida District of the Assemblies of God Chair of Board of Trustees, Southeastern University

"Having a missionary passion, Dr. Thomas Manning lives the value of transformation. In this book, *Creating Transformational Churches*, he shares not only his research but also the practical applications of his research in the churches he has led and continues to lead both in the United States and in other nations. Pastor Tom's voice encourages leaders to reignite the spiritual vitality of the local church and to formulate strategic movements toward growth and maturity. His words will inspire many to focus on those important elements needed to sustain church life in this season."

—Dr. Wayne Lee and Dr. Sherry Lee
Church Life Resources

"I love books reading books written by local church practitioners. Leaders who have dedicated a lifetime discovering and implementing church health principles into their local context. Thomas Manning is one of those leaders and *Creating Transformational Churches* is one of those books. Rich with research, *Creating Transformational Churches* also is chalked full of transferable models, divine principles and practical next steps ready to be integrated regardless of your size or context. I have had the distinct privilege of seeing this content birthed, formed and implemented at Church Life Center. This book is not a swan song to what happen years ago, but rather, it is a living document to what is happening right now at Christian Life Center. "

— Mike Harper
Church Plant and Development Director
North Texas District Council of the Assemblies of God

"In *Creating Transformational Churches*, Tom Manning lays out how Christian Life Center experienced the turnaround process. Any pastor contemplating leading their church through the turnaround process will find many helpful insights and strategies to guide them. The author also demonstrates that to really experience true turnaround, you must put into place processes that enable the transformation to become the new reality."

—J. Melvyn Ming, D.Min. D.D.
Leadership & Church Health Consultant
Leadership Development Resources, LLC

"If you are a church leader looking for ways to reignite growth in your church, then the book, *Creating Transformational Churches: A Guide to Reignite Your Church's Growth*, is a must-read. Written by Dr. Thomas Manning, this book sets out practical steps every leader can take to restore organizational health and renew the Church with fresh, Spirit-filled biblical insights. With this comprehensive guide, you can learn how to advance God's purposes and spark life-changing transformation in your local church ministry."

Dr. Rich Wilkerson and Dr. Robyn Wilkerson
Co-Pastors of Trinity Church Miami, FL.
Founders of Peacemakers

"We should expect that the Lord of the church will send help in our challenging times of leadership; I believe He has given us a gift in this time when statistics show that approximately 80 percent of churches have either plateaued or find themselves in decline. In his work, Dr. Thomas Manning has brought together research and success in the pastorate as he walks the church along the journey that he advocates in *Creating Transformational Churches*. The leader is helped to look inward, be renewed, identify the components of strong leadership, and then lead a church into a new lifecycle. Manning communicates a biblical step-by-step journey to the congregation, to revitalize spiritually, detecting and developing their own ministries to eventually work in leadership. In this time when so many leaders are complaining about the negative impact of COVID-19 on their churches, there is help for renewed vision and mission. If you are a leader serious about revitalizing for indigenous community impact, I highly recommend this book, *Creating Transformational Churches*."

—Bishop David Ewen
First Presiding Bishop, Assemblies of God Jamaica
Senior Pastor, Faith Tabernacle AG, Savanna-La-Mar,
Westmoreland, Jamaica

"Dr. Thomas Manning has availed himself of the opportunity to serve as a pacesetter over these many years of ministry. This book shows us his heart for church growth and maturity in the body of Christ. *Creating Transformational Churches* is sure to light a flame in the hearts of pastors and congregations across the world. This is a must read for all pastors—and please, the power is in implementing these principles. Thanks, Dr. Manning. This is a gift to the Body of Christ."

—Bishop Michael Grant
Former General Superintendent, Jamaica Assemblies of God
Missions Director, Jamaica Assemblies of God
Senior Pastor, Evangel Tabernacle, Old Harbour, Jamaica

"At First Assembly of God of the Cayman Islands, we have implemented several of the recommendations found in *Creating Transformational Churches*, and we are seeing a difference. This book is a must read for all pastors and church leaders."

—Pastor Torrance Bobb
General Superintendent, Cayman Islands
Senior Pastor, First Assembly of God, Cayman Islands

"I have had the privilege of coaching with Dr. Manning and witnessing firsthand the design and implementation of the principles he so adequately lays out in this book. They work! *Creating Transformational Churches* is a must read for leaders guiding congregations through the lifecycles of church health and growth."

— Duke Matlock
Executive Coach and President, Invest Leadership Initiative

"*Creating Transformational Churches* is a highly engaging and practical look at developing people in our churches. Tom shares firsthand experience of how he and Candi led Christian Life Center into a new paradigm of engaging with people on their first visit and helping them on their journey toward ministry in the church. I recommend *Creating Transformational Churches* for pastors looking to make strategic shifts in the effectiveness of their churches."

— Joey Ellis
Lead Pastor, Stone Edge Church Macon, Ga.

Dedication

I dedicate this book to my wife of thirty-three years, Candi Manning, for whom I am constantly—and eternally—grateful. This book was our life—one that she embraced, lived and breathed. She patiently listened to ideas and findings and helped build the church God had called us to lead. I will forever remain thankful for her love, support, and commitment.

Acknowledgments

I remain indebted to several people for the outcome of this book. I'm thankful for those who have encouraged and inspired me to see this through to completion.

First, I want to express appreciation for Mike Harper, who embraced the vision to bring Church Life Resources to Europe to assist the pastors of the Fellowship of European International Churches. He encouraged Dr. Wayne Lee to test the universal principles outlined by Church Life Resources through this group of passionate servants. I'm grateful that Doc Lee invited me to join his consultants' cohort through the Assemblies of God doctoral program. My ministry will forever be impacted by Doc Lee and Church Life Resources. Doc Lee provided mentoring, consultation, and inspiration for the vision in my life, and I would not have embarked on this journey if it were not for his encouragement.

I deeply appreciate the pastors, staff, board, and members of Christian Life Center (CLC) for their support and patience as I pulled away for periods of time to conduct research and write. Most importantly, however, I want to thank the church for embracing God's vision for the future, for going on a journey of change, and for aggressively implementing God's divine urgencies. Together, we have witnessed the creation of a new lifecycle and have learned the process of revitalization. I pray that we will continuously be brought back to the change points that produce new life, growth, and vitality. I love being your pastor!

And most importantly, I give thanks to the Lord Jesus Christ for His love, grace, and mercy in my life. He has given me vision, passion, anointing, and strength to fulfill His divine purposes.

About the Author

Tom Manning serves as the Senior Pastor of Christian Life Center (CLC), Fort Lauderdale, FL, a church that reaches over 5,000 attendees on a regular basis. CLC currently has five campuses across South Florida/USA and two partnering churches in the Cayman Islands.

In addition, Tom is World Missions Director for the Peninsular Florida District of the Assemblies of God—a district giving over $16 million to world missions annually. He also served as a General Presbyter for the Assemblies of God.

Previously, Tom and his wife, Candi, served as missionaries with the Assemblies of God in Budapest, Hungary, and as Senior Pastors of Vienna Christian Center (VCC) in Austria from 2000-2012. VCC consists of over sixty nationalities, has twelve-weekend services in seven different languages and locations, and reaches over 2,500 weekly.

Pastor Tom is a consultant with Church Life Resources, working with hundreds of pastors and churches annually. He completed his Master of Divinity in Church Growth and Renewal and his Doctor of Ministry (D.Min.) in Church Health and Revitalization. He has held pastors training seminars and conventions in Italy, Austria, Croatia, Singapore, Romania, Cayman Islands, Hungary, Belgium, United Kingdom, Spain, France, Cuba, Belize, Antigua, Colombia, Curacao, Bahamas, USVI, Suriname, Columbia, and Jamaica.

Tom and his wife, Candi, have three sons—Jonathan (wife Stephanie), Christopher, and Andrew. They love boating, traveling, and working with pastors and leaders from around the world.

Foreword

"We can't stay here!"

It's been several years now since those words first pierced my spirit. Challenged with the assignment to help hundreds of congregations still trying to battle their ever-changing landscapes with status quo efforts that long ago had lost their effectiveness, I knew then that something simply had to change, and that feeling has never faded in its intensity. Reminded of God's words to Moses, "You have dwelt long enough at this mountain," I daily find myself desperate to help pastors and church leaders let go of mundane realities that have trapped them and find real paths to the new days that they and their congregations desperately need.

Those same words continue to drive me even now, and frankly, there's never been a greater need for change in thousands of America's local churches. As my friend, Tom Manning, highlights in the pages of this book, the decline of local churches in America has reached epidemic proportions. Culture continues and has even escalated its determined march away from the Christian worldview that once marked its foundations, while the local church has largely been banished as a traditional and unwanted voice that no longer speaks to its times. Other religions and rising secularism now claim equal rights to the hearts of people who once considered themselves "one nation under God." Truth itself is up for grabs, and any suggestion of natural law or appropriate morality is quickly and even angrily dismissed. Add recent crises that made even our existing efforts impossible for a time, and you find an almost perfect storm of difficulty that many congregations failed to survive while others were left to limp noticeably into their uncertain tomorrows. Clearly, something must change, and, as we all know, change has never really been the local church's specialty.

But there is hope. Against the harsh backdrop of such modern realities are congregations finding their way forward—with many even leaving deep footprints with every step. These have found answers, not on the cutting edge of the latest fashionable ideas but in a determined return to their original mission and the focus and power that launched the Church itself centuries ago. Their methods look different, but their mission remains firm. Their eyes are set on a vision for the future that is proving more powerful than what others see as insurmountable limitations. They, like their spiritual ancestors in the Church's first century, are living Jesus's determined promise to build His Church despite all odds, and in the face of the greatest resistance hell can muster.

I've seen local churches at their best reach even higher. I've watched as seemingly average folks have climbed beyond their own capacities into places where only God's Spirit could lead them. I've worshipped alongside the Spirit-empowered and celebrated the life-changing journeys that continue to emerge in their midst. How is this possible? It's the mission and the power of the One who gave it.

No, we can't stay here, and the Spirit of God is determined that we won't if we will renew our passion for His plans in our communities. Every single one of us is called to His mission to "make disciples" of all nations, and I'm grateful for every story where folks are engaging in this priority assignment. I also rejoice in the dozens of others who have rolled up their sleeves to help congregations around the globe move from marching in circles to chasing God's greater dreams. In the pages that follow, Tom Manning has combined many of their insights with those he discovered himself in the journey that transformed both him and his congregation at Christian Life Center (CLC). Today, CLC is a congregation effectively producing disciples and making an impact in their community and beyond.

Something must change … in many more places. We simply can't stay here!

—Alton Garrison
Executive Director, Acts 2 Journey
Former Assistant General Superintendent of the Assemblies of
God USA

Preface

Statistics indicate that over 80 percent of churches have plateaued or suffered a decline. Within time and without intervention, these churches will die as they follow the natural flow of the organizational lifecycle. However, churches do not have to experience the final stages of the organizational lifecycle because they possess a potential for renewed growth. Pastors can learn the art of leading a church through revitalization, advancing God's purposes, restoring health, and renewing the church to pulsate with the dynamic presence of Christ.

This book will explain that which brings life and transformation to the local church. I will explain the transformational process that tackles the decline experienced by churches and that which brings substantial growth. I will walk the reader through the development of a comprehensive plan that identifies immediate urgencies and steps needed to break restricting behaviors and hindrances and outline the necessary steps to renewing health and fostering growth in the church.

My goal is to help demonstrate the creation of a new lifecycle using a biblical, comprehensive, Spirit-filled approach, one that works systemically and developmentally for churches of any size. To provide for every pastor and leader a guide to transformational growth that creates new life in the church and an impact in the community.

Introduction

In 1988, Win Arn shocked church leaders with his statistics that four out of five churches remain plateaued or declining. He explained that "many churches begin a plateau or slow decline about their fifteenth to eighteenth year."[1] Research shows that this trend has continued. Church attendance continues to decline, especially as young people leave their local churches. Aubrey Malphurs and Gordon Penfold claim that "the church in America faces great challenges. Most churches are plateaued or declining in worship attendance. The percentage of people attending church is shrinking, and young people eighteen to twenty-nine are abandoning the faith."[2] This information factually reinforces what churches and pastors inherently experience across the nation.

The Purpose

The purpose of this book is to share a transformational process that will address the decline in local churches and show how to create a new lifecycle.

Churches naturally go through ups and downs, victory and defeat, joy and sorrow. Like every other type of organization, churches have a predictable lifecycle, one inclined to follow basic patterns of growth, plateau, and decline. When a church leader knows what stage of the lifecycle one's church is experiencing, the leader will develop a clearer understanding of the strategies involved in renewing the lifecycle of the church. While many churches experience the problem of plateau or decline, they also have the opportunity to create a new lifecycle. This book will demonstrate the necessary elements for creating a new lifecycle in the church that creates growth and vitality.

Definition of Terms

Church Revitalization—the process of bringing life and growth to a church in plateau or decline.

Lifecycle—the series of changes in the life of an organism or organization. Organisms and organizations are born, then grow, age, and die.

New Lifecycle in a Church—renewed vision, health, spiritual vitality, authentic relationships, increase in volunteerism, increase in leaders, financial health, and community impact.

Process—a series of actions or steps taken to achieve a particular end.

Transformational—a thorough and dramatic change in one's spirituality, authentic connections, growth, and service within the church and community.

Church Life Model – a model derived from the New Testament identifying both the global and specific components of the church.

Chapter 1
The State of the Church

In 2014, Thom Rainer, an expert consultant on the state of the church in North America, said 80 percent "of the approximately 400,000 churches in the United States are declining or have plateaued," and as many as 100,000 churches show signs of decline toward death.[1] David Olson's research in *The State of the American Church* estimates that 84 percent of churches experience growth below the population growth rate, which indicates a plateaued church.[2]

The American Church has sounded the call
for revitalization.

Although church involvement once stood as a cornerstone of American life, U.S. adults today remain evenly divided on the importance of attending church. While half (49 percent) say attendance is "somewhat" or "very" important, the other 51 percent maintain that it is "not too" or "not at all" important.[3] The divide between the religiously active and those resistant to churchgoing impacts American culture, morality, politics, and religion.

Olson's research indicates that on any given weekend, only 17 percent of the US population attends church; this figure includes Catholic, Evangelical, mainline, and Orthodox churches.[4] In comparison to the population of the United States, which increased by 24 percent from 1990 to 2010, church attendance remained virtually unchanged during this same time period.[5] According to the Assemblies of God, worship attendance has increased only .5 percent since 2004.[6] In numerous studies by the Barna Research Group, fewer Americans than ever attend church; however, many of these people do not reject spirituality; they reject the contemporary church.[7] In their recent book *Re:Vision*, Aubrey Malphurs, and Gordon Penfold claim that "the church in America faces great challenges. Most churches are plateaued or declining in worship attendance. The percentage of people attending church is shrinking, and young people eighteen to twenty-nine are abandoning the faith."[8]

David Kinnaman agrees with these findings:

> The ages of eighteen to twenty-nine are the black hole of church attendance; this age segment is "missing in action" from most congregations. ... Overall, there is a 43% drop-off between the teen and early adult years in terms of church engagement. These numbers represent about 8 million twenty something's who were active churchgoers as teenagers who will no longer be a part of or currently engaged in the church by their thirtieth birthday.[9]

The decline has occurred in churches of every denomination in the past twenty years.[10]

The statistics remain alarming, prompting many to explore the issue of church renewal, church growth, church health, revival, and awakening—simply, the American Church has sounded the call for revitalization. This book examines issues relevant to creating new lifecycles within the contemporary church. The research focuses on the following topics: (1) lifecycles of an organization, (2) the

4

revitalization of the Pentecostal Church, and (3) the transformational process to creating a new lifecycle.

The Lifecycle of An Organization

A lifecycle is the discernable pattern to life. The lifecycles of organizations and churches comprise four stages: birth, development, maturity, and decline. Ichak Adizes popularized the concept of organizational lifecycles in his book *Corporate Lifecycles: How and Why Corporations Grow and Die and What to Do about It*. Much like the human lifecycle, Adizes identifies four stages of growth within an organization and four stages of decline: growth includes courtship, infant, go-go, and adolescence, while decline includes aristocracy, early bureaucracy (Recrimination), bureaucracy, and death. In addition to these eight stages, he identifies two other stages of being: prime and stable. He places stable (also referred to as the "fall") at the top of the bell curve and places prime just before the top. Stable describes the beginning of a plateau in the lifecycle, which results in the movement toward decline. During stability, an organization loses

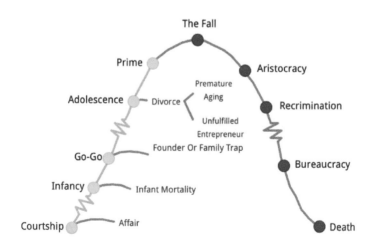

vision, creativity, and innovation, and it begins its decline, as seen below in Adizes's Organizational Lifecycle Model:

Adizes identifies prime as the ideal stage of an organization:

> In Prime, the organization knows what to do and what not to do. They know when to pass up an opportunity and why to pass on it. The organization has both talent and discipline. It has vision and self-control. It is oriented toward quantity and quality. Both form and function are balanced, and they are functional. The organization can grow profitably.[11]

The major goal of any organization, according to Adizes, consists of achieving prime; the second goal strives to stay or return to prime.

Lifecycles of organizations and churches comprise four
stages: birth, development, maturity,
and decline.

Robert D. Dale popularized the lifecycle concept among church leaders. Dale models his church lifecycle on that of human development. His nine stages of the church's life include beliefs, goals, structure, ministry, nostalgia, questioning, polarization, and dropout.[12] Martin Saarinen and George W. Bullard Jr. used Adizes's research to develop similar congregational lifecycle models that inform growth and decline. Saarinen focuses on the points and risk factors for congregations at each stage.[13] This is helpful for evaluating a church's current lifecycle. In addition, George Bullard's model of congregational development provides the tools and identifying questions that assess factors contributing to a church's decline.[14] He breaks down the constant change of a church's lifecycle into ten stages of congregational development, which occurs within five

6

lifecycle phases: early growth, late growth, prime/plateau, early aging, and late aging.[15]

Life Cycle Stages of a Church

Phase 3: Prime/Plateau

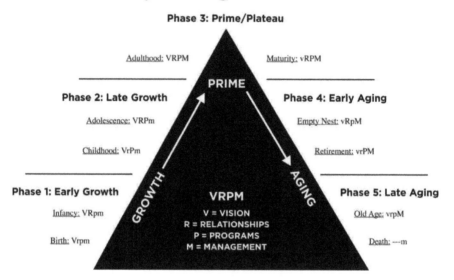

Adulthood: VRPM   Maturity: vRPM

PRIME

Phase 2: Late Growth   **Phase 4: Early Aging**

Adolescence: VRPm   Empty Nest: vRpM

Childhood: VrPm   Retirement: vrPM

Phase 1: Early Growth   VRPM   **Phase 5: Late Aging**

Infancy: VRpm   V = VISION   Old Age: vrpM
                       R = RELATIONSHIPS
Birth: Vrpm   P = PROGRAMS   Death: ---m
                       M = MANAGEMENT

GROWTH   AGING

Bullard's model offers the most helpful grid for analyzing the current status of a church's lifecycle. As he describes how churches pass through each stage, he describes each stage's characteristics and agendas. As a church ages, it can get comfortable in how things have always been done and lose sight of one of the key foundations that keep it alive – vision, relationships, programs, and management. As Alton Garrison explains, "Once the church reaches maturity, if there is not intentional and continuous vision casting, relationship building, and ministry growth, the church tends to move from the ascending side of the lifecycle to the descending side."[16]

Bullard reminds us that the transformation journey is an ongoing process. In his words, "Congregations who continually transform hardwire into their culture the process of always engaging in transition and change."[17]

As we look at his model, we see how churches come to a crossroad where they either need to find ways to continue to grow, or they decline and possibly die.

In particular, his explanation of old age and death remains highly informative as it pertains to the current state of the American Church. In the description of his model, Bullard explores a stage not identified in the diagram—resurrection—a stage he entitles "organ donation."[18] This is what takes place when a congregation has experienced death, yet they find new life in a different format. Bullard says this can occur in a variety of situations, such as

1. Another congregation can purchase the facilities and provide Christian ministry to the community targeted by the former congregation.
2. The resources of the former congregation can be used to give life to another congregation.
3. A remnant from the former congregation can be part of the Birth of a new congregation.
4. Their denomination can use the financial asset of the former congregation to start new congregations.[19]

Both Saarinen and Bullard borrow largely from Adizes in their work but present fresh ideas and label stages to fit congregations while remaining aligned with Adizes's perspectives.

Bullard's model also incorporates helpful characteristics represented by letters to indicate church status: vision (V), relationship (R), program (P), and management (M). Capitalized letters indicate strong development of a characteristic at any given stage; lowercase letters indicate weaker development. In Bullard's model, adulthood remains the ideal stage within the lifecycle.[20]

Gary McIntosh, a nationally known church growth expert, also asserts that churches follow similar patterns of corporate growth and decline. He notes that

> congregations tend to traverse a predictable life cycle that is similar to a bell curve. A church is prone to rapid growth in the first fifteen to twenty years of its existence, followed by a leveling off of growth onto a plateau for another twenty to forty years. Then follows a slower decline over the next thirty to forty years until the church either closes its doors (dies) or eases into an unhealthy period of stagnation.[21]

David O. Moberg, the first to popularize lifecycle thinking for churches, notes that "the process by which an institution develops may be called its natural history and has a typical pattern through which they pass as they emerge, grow, decline, and ultimately die."[22] He calls this unhealthy stagnation "institutionalization;" as an organization grows, it moves through phases, which are characterized by mounting bureaucracy, eventually becoming less effective and collapsing under its own weight.[23]

While Dale, Saarinen, Bullard, McIntosh, and Moberg all describe the lifecycle of the church in various and informative ways, all ultimately do agree that local churches experience a predictable lifecycle of growth and decline. Most conclude that a church's lifecycle, which Arnold Cook calls the historical drift, encompasses approximately fifty years.[24] Although some travel along the lifecycle faster or slower, eventually, all follow the same basic pattern and have similar causes for plateau and decline.

Chapter 2

Major Causes for Plateau

and Decline

Churches share common characteristics as they pass from one stage to another. These characteristics, which describe their internal cultures, behavior, and processes, offer clues into assessing how long an organization will likely thrive. The lifecycle models of Adizes, Dale, Saarinen, Bullard, Moberg, and McIntosh, all illustrate how organizations and churches remain inclined to follow a basic pattern of growth, plateau, and decline. McIntosh clarifies that in seeking to assess the health of a church, leaders must understand that what brings

> a church to its current level of ministry fruitfulness will not get it to the next level of growth and vitality. Leaders learn quickly that as a church grows and ages, it becomes increasingly difficult to keep it healthy and vibrant. Over time, people change, conflicts build, and programs peak in effectiveness. Long-term excellence is always the result of continual improvements over time.[1]

Without such long-term excellence and continual improvement, most decline in churches eventually leads to closure. Churches lose members, income, energy, vision, and the ability to minister in a changing world. Unless they reverse those dynamics, death will inevitably occur. George Barna lists several symptoms that may indicate a church in decline: demographic changes, inadequate leadership, poor management, old blood, building campaigns, the ingrown family, resistance to change, and spiritual health.[2] These symptoms discussed later in this chapter, can be placed into six major categories: leadership/vision, spiritual life, spiritual community, ministry/discipleship, outreach, and management/ structure.

Two primary reasons contribute to church decline: (1) leaders do not know what a disciple looks like, nor do they have a clearly defined picture of God's purpose for their churches and what God calls them to produce; (2) leaders do not know how to intentionally produce disciples with a clear purpose.[3] Understanding a church's purpose (or mission) provides a biblical reason for church ministry; its vision provides energy, hope, and passion. McIntosh believes that "when a church and its leaders lose a sense of vision, the ministry starts winding down."[4] This lack of visionary leadership and lack of clear purpose remain primary issues for many churches in decline today.

A lack of visionary leadership and clear purpose remain
primary issues for many churches
in decline today.

Malphurs and Penfold also link the major cause of decline to pastoral leadership, poor pastoral preparation, and too-high expectations placed on pastors by the church membership.[5] Believing that many pastors lack the proper preparation for pastoral leadership, they note that typical pastoral training programs prepare pastors "to do book management and perform religious rights, instead of developing people. This shift will lead to a lower involvement in the local church by church membership, who will shift their commitments to people and causes beyond the church."[6] Since visionary leadership remains at the core of church life, an emphasis on leading healthy congregations is necessary for church revitalization. In this context,

Malphurs and Penfold have developed four critical questions pastors can ask themselves to help them determine whether to have a role in leading a church through revitalization: "What if I'm a re-envisioning pastor? What if I'm a non-re-envisioning pastor? Can a non-re-envisioning pastor become a re-envisioning pastor? ... [and] Should a non-re-envisioning pastor become a re-envisioning pastor?"[7] Malphurs and Penfold conclude that God does not divinely design all pastors with the gifts, passion, and temperament to lead a church to revitalize.

The need for church revitalization
remains enormous.

The need for church revitalization remains enormous, especially since many young people are not responding to the call of God. A shortage of visionary pastors exists, those capable of leading a church to embrace the necessary change that will create a new lifecycle. Pastors must learn the skill of developing and casting a vision that others will embrace. Churches without a clear, God-inspired vision will remain fruitless because they will fail to articulate what God has called the Church to do. Those who sense a call and desire to embark on the journey of church revitalization will find Malphurs's and Penfold's re-envisioning curriculum beneficial.[8]

Complicating this problem is a change in society, which adds to the decline in churches. Congregants "no longer look to or rely on the clergy and church leaders to script or dictate their spiritual and personal development."[9] With the ease of Internet streaming and archiving of messages, spiritual development becomes increasingly disconnected to any one spiritual leader, pastor, or church. Many people receive their spiritual growth daily through blogs, emails, podcasts, and online media.

As noted earlier, the American Church continues to lose members, especially young adults, at an ever-increasing rate. One major reason for this loss concerns the church's lack of relevance to modern culture. Olson notes that churches that do not adjust to changes in the culture will struggle:

> Although the gospel message should not change, a church needs to find new methods and styles of communication—in art, music, dialogue, and preaching—that truly engage people in the community … Many churches mistake culturally bound ministry styles for core theology. For many churches, their music, stories, programs, and means of community outreach no longer resonate with those outside of their church. A generation can become "culture-bound" and not notice they are increasingly out of touch with the changes. It is always easy for a generation to see the flaws in the previous generation yet miss their own shortcomings.[10]

Many churches do not know or realize the danger they face until it is too late. Before hitting their plateau, they operate on autopilot, "coasting and admiring past victories, which lead to organizational inertia."[11] This organizational inertia characterizes the fall in Adizes's model, which begins when the church passes prime and enters stable (plateau). Since plateau sits at the apex, the institutional situation appears secure; however, this "quiet time and organizational life is really the lull before the storm."[12]

Malphurs and Penfold assert that the first step to addressing a decline is to examine the reality of the current situation in the local

13

church. This examination begins by checking the vital signs of the church, basic things such as worship attendance, giving, strengths, and weaknesses.[13] A helpful tool used by the Malphurs Group to help churches see their need for revitalization consists of sixteen make-or-break questions:[14]

1. Do you have your finger on the church's pulse so that you can regularly read your critical vital signs?
2. Do you have a contagious, memorable mission that serves as a compass to navigate your church through whitewater change? Does it roll off your tongue with clarity and conviction?
3. Do you habitually consult your mission statement when making any and all decisions that affect the future direction of your church?
4. Have you carefully identified your actual core values so that you understand why you are successful in some areas and struggle in others, such as evangelism?
5. Has your church's impact on your community been such that if you were to suddenly disappear, it would leave a serious hole in your community?
6. Do your people view themselves as merely the church's members or Christ's missionaries?
7. Do you have a clear, simple pathway for making disciples that most in your church understand and know where they are on that path?
8. Does your staff team enthusiastically align with your core values, mission, and vision?
9. Do you have an intentional process for increasing and empowering lay volunteers to lead and do the church's ministries?
10. Do you have a staffing blueprint that provides crystal clarity about the next ministry to launch and who will lead it?

11. Do your facilities contribute functionally to the realization of your vision in the community?
12. Do you have a biblical strategy in place for raising finances that has resulted in an increase in giving over the last few years in spite of the recession?
13. Does your church's vision cast a clear, compelling picture of your future? In the last thirty days, have you overheard a church member articulate or discuss your vision?
14. Do you have an intentional process for developing key leaders at every level in your church? Can you outline it on a napkin over a cup of coffee?
15. Have you crafted a personal, individualized leader development plan for your own growth as a leader in your church?
16. Has your pastor or anyone on staff identified and enlisted a coach to help him or her grow and stay fresh as a leader?

These questions are articulated in such a way that most leaders will realize that they have substantial work to do to keep the church in its prime and out of plateau.

Every church will experience times in their lifecycle when God intervenes with opportunities for the church to seize. These "divine interruptions" are easy to recognize when a church remains alert and understands its vision and mission in Christ.[15] Malphurs and Penfold list five possible interruptions: (1) a crisis, (2) a change of pastors, (3) a renewal of the pastor, (4) a renewal of lay leadership, and (5) the expertise of a church consultant or mentor.[16] Ultimately, a variety of opportunities and factors impact the revitalization of a Pentecostal congregation, but more importantly, the process of creating a new lifecycle begins with the transformation of the leader.

Chapter 3

The Process of Transformation

The process of transformation for a Pentecostal congregation involves the transformation of the leader, the congregation's spiritual life, spiritual community, spiritual formation, development and release of spiritual gifts, missional effectiveness, and the management/structure within the church. This process of transformation will effect change that leads to paradigm shifts and revitalization of a congregation.

Transformation of the Leader

The most important aspect of revitalization for a congregation is the transformation of the local pastor. Transformation affects character, leadership qualities, traits, characteristics, personality, gifts, calling, and passions.[1] Stetzer and Dobson research indicate that churches that have experienced revitalization first experienced some type of change or transformation within the pastoral leadership. They note, "the reason for a change in pastoral leadership is that these churches needed change in general, … [and as these churches persist] in a pattern of plateau and decline," only those pastors who willingly change or renew themselves will successfully lead a church in revitalization.[2] Olson agrees on the importance of the transformation of the leader: "Pastors are severely limited in their leadership effectiveness unless they know how to lead authentically."[3] This leadership authenticity comes from learning how to lead effectively, which then becomes part of the transformational path for the revitalization of the church. Transformation begins with the pastor, which then impacts the church. Unfortunately, many pastors do not realize the integral role they have and simply believe that the plateau or decline of their churches stems from reasons other than themselves. Most often, however, the reality is that the pastor/leader remains a core part of the issue.

Personal spiritual renewal remains the key
to creating a new lifecycle.

A leader's transformation begins with spiritual renewal through prayer, renewed devotion, waiting, and discerning. The leader must experience God in authentic moments in His presence while reading Scripture, praying, practicing solitude, fasting, contemplation, intercession, and meditation. Brian McLaren says the church needs "leadership by personal authenticity … [from leaders who] look at the tasks and qualities demanded."[4] Personal spiritual renewal remains the key to creating a new lifecycle. Transformation in the pastor leads to church transformation, which empowers the pastor to lead the congregation to spiritual health and vitality. Fresh experiences, new encounters, and a spiritual renewing of one's calling come through these divine encounters with the living God. Learning to replenish spiritually is a necessity.

Revitalization also requires strong visionary leadership. A pastor who can turn around a church learns to "make the right decisions for the right reasons. They're able to design a plan for the comeback that makes sense and [that] the people will accept."[5] The challenge, however, is that few churches have this type of strong visionary leadership. Malphurs and Penfold claim there is "not necessarily a lack of leaders. Churches are rarely developing visionary leaders."[6]

Visionary leaders understand the biblical nature, tasks, and responsibilities of leadership and the need for constant intentional focus on the mission of Christ. Visionary leadership develops in churches, training programs, seminars and conferences, seminaries, and Bible schools—and through mentorship and coaching. Pastors need a development plan that addresses key areas: character, personality, calling, abilities, knowledge, emotional intelligence, skills, and roles.

Visionary leaders also understand the need for a clear and compelling vision in transformation and revitalization.

Wayne and Sherry Lee of Church Life Resources have developed a useful diagram for understanding the process of developing strong leaders. They identify three main components of strong leadership: personhood, roles, and execution. The first component, personhood, addresses the development of a leader's personal and spiritual life. Personhood stresses the importance of character, personality, calling, passion, mission, and vision. The second component, roles, addresses the functions and responsibilities of leadership. Roles include providing visionary leadership, supplying spiritual leadership and communication, being the spiritual community developer and caregiver, directing ministry and discipleship, overseeing outreach, and managing resources. The third component, execution of leadership, requires the ability to discern urgencies and realities, formulate teams and strategies, empower team implementation, and recognize the transformational activity of God.[7]

Undergirding these three main components are strong personal and spiritual formation, the continual pursuit of knowledge, healthy practice, and accountability with mentors to provide continual reflection, along with God-given anointing, authority, and influence. Finally, all these characteristics, roles, and components must remain continually informed by an acute awareness of personal and spiritual weaknesses, the dark side of leadership.[8]

Visionary leaders also understand the need for a clear and compelling vision in transformation and revitalization.

They do this by "under-standing what vision is, why we need it, when to share it, how to paint the picture, how to persuade, counting the cost, and keeping the vision before the people."[9] Thom Rainer and Eric Geiger define leadership as helping "place people in the pathway of God's transforming power. To design a process that partners with the transformation process revealed in Scripture."[10] Pastors returning to God's process for making disciples "have designed a ministry process that puts people in the place for God to transform them."[11] Visionary pastors have the ability to see what God wants in a given situation and through a group of people and are able to articulate the necessary course of action to see the vision fulfilled. Mark Rutland asserts that the "turnaround leader is the Chief Culture Officer in an organization, ... [the person who will] create a vision and communicate that vision at every opportunity to every person who will stand still or walk slow."[12]

The missional thrust of the Church comes as God releases the impulses of divine mission and vision to His body. God charges pastors with facilitating the mission of Christ through the church, while vision is a statement of what God will do. Rutland describes how vision takes root in the heart of God's people:

19

When leaders first can see possibilities for the future, they are like everyone else—dreaming of a better tomorrow. But somewhere along the line, something more happens. God begins to impart faith to the leader. The dream matures and becomes more culture. Through prayer, the leader gives God access to the dream he holds in his heart. God then speaks to the leader by breathing faith into those parts of the dream that reflect God's plan for the local church he leads. This faith makes the vision seem real and attainable. To those looking on, the vision seems unreachable at first, but when the leader speaks and shares his heart on the matter, faith acts like a contagion—others begin to believe that the impossible is now possible.[13]

According to George Barna, people want a leader but will only follow someone they deem worthy: "In essence, they will refuse to place their trust and future in the hands of an alleged leader who does not possess vision."[14]

The key to revitalization is not just shared vision; it is "the connection between the dream, its proclamation, and making the dream the driving force of everything that is done."[15] Transformational leaders learn to discern the divine impulses of that which is to be activated in the local church. God speaks, and Pentecostal leaders must under-stand and communicate His divine message to the church.

Malphurs and Penfold have found, however, that many pastors lack the ability to articulate a vision for the church. They have not been trained to see the dream, save the dream, or share the dream; they remain "bricklayers rather than architects."[16] The leader must consistently reinforce the vision for the people, making it easier to remember and live it by "continually reminding them in creative, appealing, and meaningful ways."[17]

John Kotter, in his classic work, *Leading Change*, stresses that leaders must communicate vision in order to see transformation: "The people will not make sacrifices, even if they are unhappy with the status quo unless they think the potential benefits of change are attractive and unless they really believe that a transformation is possible."[18] Rutland reinforces this point: "The vision gets fractured, scattered, and twisted as it goes down through the ranks. It loses power and focus. You have to gather all those pieces up and speak them again with fresh energy. Speak the vision with enthusiasm and vitality every time, as if it's the most fascinating thing you've ever said."[19] Rutland, having led several turnaround organizations, understands how vision sticks and what it takes to create renewed momentum.

The revitalization of a local church requires the focus and commitment of leaders who serve as agents of change and transformation.

"If a church is to capture the heart of its community, Christ must first capture the heart of the pastor. Revitalization leaders live the mission."[20] This transformation always begins with the pastor.

Transformation of the Spiritual Life of the Congregation

Balanced spiritual vitality thrusts a congregation into its mission and vision. Revitalization primarily remains a spiritual issue, and it occurs when the body of Christ engages in activities that bring them into an awareness of the presence of God. Churches create a new lifecycle by prioritizing the spiritual life of the congregation by emphasizing spiritual disciplines such as prayer, fasting, corporate worship, and private devotions. Richard Foster categorizes spiritual disciplines into (1) the inward disciplines, which include meditation, prayer, fasting, and study, (2) the outward disciplines of simplicity, solitude, submission, and service, and (3) the corporate disciplines of confession, worship, guidance, and celebration.[21] Practicing these disciplines both individually and corporately maximizes spirituality within the church. In his research, John Larue discovered that 75 percent of revitalized churches reported starting such spiritual discipline initiatives in their congregations.[22]

Prayer changes circumstances and
releases the supernatural.

Churches that revitalize by creating new lifecycles understand that the spiritual health and life of a congregation remain multi-dimensional; they nurture the people of God to experience His presence both privately and corporately. This gives a deep awareness of the presence of the Lord and brings a vitality that meets the church's needs, enlarges its vision, and enables it to accomplish its God-given mission. These churches remain praying churches. Revivals take place when God's people pray and when they obey God's Word. The Holy Spirit's presence and power releases through intentional prayer: "There simply is no more important principle in church growth then prayer. The prayers of the early church unleashed the power of God to add thousands to the church."[23] Prayer changes circumstances and releases the supernatural. As leaders increase the spiritual fervor of the congregation, "the church has an innate ability to renew itself spiritually."[24]

Spiritual renewal begins with the leader through prayer,
renewed devotion, waiting, and discerning.

As the church embraces God's call to return to their first love, it generates movement and arouses passion to see and know God, to connect one's heart with the Holy Spirit's present work on the earth. The believer's spirituality forms in the continuous encounter with God, which comes only through participating in the Christian disciplines: "Biblical spirituality ... is concerned with bringing our body and soul into an intimate relationship with the heart of God. It is concerned with holiness, which means that it relates to every aspect of life, as lived from day to day."[25]

The leader of revitalization needs to experience renewal before leading others to spiritual health and vitality. The pastoral leaders and a sizeable core of lay leaders must experience, model, and teach spiritual health before revitalization permeates the congregation. This spiritual renewal gives leaders a vision and provides focus, helping them develop practical and powerful plans.

The leader of revitalization needs to experience renewal
before leading others to spiritual health
and vitality.

God uses preaching and teaching to bring life change, forming the believer into Christlikeness and inspiring transformation: "the best way to revive the church is to build a fire in the pulpit."[26] This "fire in the pulpit" brings Christ-like convictions (the way believers think),

Christ-like character (the way they feel), and Christ-like conduct (the way they act). Preaching shares the "authentic revealed Word of God" in a way that changes lives and prepares God's people to build up the body of Christ.[27] The goal is to lead people to live as doers of the Word, not just hearers.

This spiritual renewal and revitalization require a reliance on the Holy Spirit to make the planted seed grow: "Fruitful ministry is a remarkable combination of God-directed human effort converging with the work of the Holy Spirit to manifest the touch of God himself … transformation is solely the work of the Holy Spirit."[28] This spiritual empowerment remains one reason churches can revitalize and thrive again.[29]

According to Rainer and Geiger, church leaders must be designers, not programmers: "Church leaders who are designers are focused on the end result, the overall picture. They are as concerned with what happens between the programs as with the programs themselves."[30] A challenge for many Pentecostal leaders lies in recognizing the true spiritual condition of the church. Without this recognition, they cannot develop a transformation process that moves people toward spiritual maturity.

Transformation of the Spiritual Community of the Congregation

A major characteristic of the body of Christ is a spiritual community, often called fellowship, care, connection, bonding, brotherly love, or *koinonia*. Spiritual community provides the "development of meaningful relationships where every member carries a significant sense of belonging."[31] The spiritual life of a congregation connects people to God, while the spiritual community connects people to one another. Spiritual community conserves the fruit of evangelism and draws believers to become members of the community, where they will receive care and fellowship. Lee and Lee contend that belonging to this "family of God" meets emotional and spiritual needs and allows the individual to "participate in the *koinonia* presence of God."[32] This belonging offers not only the presence of God as "real and wonderful," but it also "surrounds, envelops, and acknowledges the individual uniqueness of each person" and "makes the body one in Christ's love."[33]

People come to church for a variety of reasons, but they primarily stay for relationships. Growing churches remain highly intentional in designing assimilation strategies and systems that start before someone even steps foot in the church. Nelson Searcy believes assimilation can transform lives by helping people become mature Christ followers.[34] He defines this assimilation as "the process used to encourage your first-time guests to continue coming back until they see and understand God's power, accept Jesus as their Savior, and commit themselves to the local church through membership."[35] These meaningful relationships are essential "to what it means to be the church. This is a God-ordained gathering of people that is so strong that even 'the gates of hell will not overcome it.'"[36]

Pastoral care remains the responsibility of the entire church, not just the pastor.

Genuine caring best takes place in small groups, "the engine in each local church that propels its growth."[37] When people see and experience a care-giving environment, their lives change, impacting their friendship network. Everyone needs a relational network of believers; however, the relational network remains critical for new believers. Shepherding, the biblical model of caring, involves modeling, nurturing, feeding, and protecting.

Church members will disengage without consistent care.[38] The easiest way to care for everyone is to connect each person to a life group, ministry group, serving group, or outreach group that provides care by "extending friendliness, kindness, encouragement, comfort, warmth in relationships, practical assistance, companion-ship, and prayer for others."[39] This kind of pastoral care remains the responsibility of the entire church, not just the pastor: "If a church relies solely on the pastoral staff to provide care for all church members, it will fail. The only practical way to provide care is to give every person in the church this responsibility. If everyone is involved in caring for each other, there is high probability that the care provided will be good and consistent."[40]

A church must have a deep commitment to fulfilling the great commandment to create a new lifecycle.

Congregants will build relational, transforming communities where people experience oneness with God and oneness with one another, "communities that are so satisfying, so unique, and so compelling that they create thirst in a watching world."[41] As a biblical mandate, spiritual leaders must connect people in the community in such a way as to "unwrap God's gifts of oneness among his people."[42] People need connection, and churches that revitalize use strategies that help people stay and grow. Getting people to come and visit is one thing; getting them to stay is another challenge altogether. Neither is easy, but both remain necessary.

Transformation of the Spiritual Formation of the Congregation

In His final words to the disciples, Jesus says, "Go and make disciples of all nations baptizing them in the name of the Father, the Son and the Holy Spirit, and teaching them to do everything I have commanded you" (Matt 28:18-20). Churches that create new lifecycles develop a system of discipleship, giving prominent attention to the growth and maturity of members. This process, often referred to as spiritual formation, promotes growth and establishes strength within the members so the body moves, grows, and fulfills the vision and mission of God. The goal or mission of discipleship is to make disciples—teach, train, and equip them—so they, in turn, can fulfill the Great Commission.

The goal of every Christian must be
to become like Christ, a goal the
church must support.

Churches should ensure that each member receives teaching on the key habits of discipleship: reading Scripture, prayer, small groups, tithing, witnessing, and other disciplines. While numerous topics seem more desirable to learn (e.g., end times, spiritual warfare, etc.), believers must first learn the basic disciplines of the Christian life. Maturity in Christ occurs through encounters with God, hearing and receiving the Word, exercising spiritual gifts, becoming involved in ministry, and evangelizing others. The goal of every Christian must be to become like Christ, a goal the church must support. Despite this need, Geiger and Rainer have found that most churches "have not designed a simple process for discipleship. They have not structured their church around the process of spiritual transformation. And they are making little impact."[43]

Spiritual formation requires an intentional strategy designed around a straightforward and strategic process that moves people through the stages of spiritual growth.

A major barrier to growth in many churches comes from the lack of a simple discipleship process. Growing churches not only have a clear discipleship process, they ensure the process is streamlined.[44] Spiritual leaders who revitalize churches help the church understand goals and remain clear about the process. Below is the discipleship process instituted at CLC. See chapter 6, "The Process of Making Disciples" for an overview of the CLC Discipleship Process and chapters 7-10, which address the four phases: Share, Connect, Train, and Release. In the SHARE phase, people *experience God*. In the CONNECT phase, they are *connecting together* with other believers. In the TRAIN phase, they are *growing and serving*. In the RELEASE phase, they are *impacting* our world.

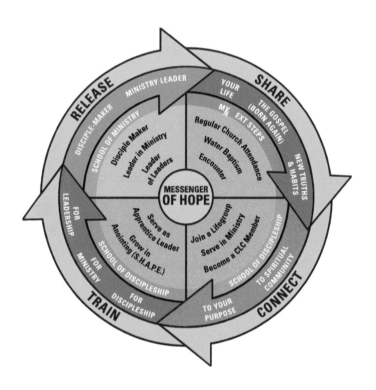

29

The following graphic details these four phases further:

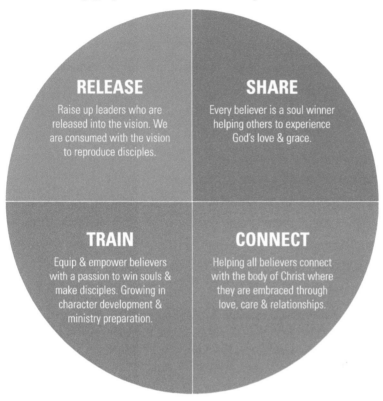

Who we are as Messengers of Hope leads us to what we do: Share, Connect, Train and Release. Creating this environment is the work of the pastor and the leadership.

Andy Stanley affirms that revitalizing leaders are "clear about the process" and "are committed to executing it;" they make sure the "process flows logically," is "implemented in each area of the church," and they make sure the church remains focused.[45] This process yields the power of transformation. Leaders must answer the question of where people should go, which clarifies the win for the organization: "Regrettably, many churches are not clear on what a win looks like for them, so they don't know how to go about achieving the win."[46]

Geiger and Rainer found that 54 percent of vibrant churches intentionally place programs to work in conjunction with ministry process, compared to 30 percent of non-growing churches; however, the "sequential programming is vital."[47] Offering a clearly defined next step to the spiritual transformation process proves essential: "Vibrant churches are more than twice as likely as the comparison churches to offer a clear next step to new believers"[48] With regard to implementation, Geiger and Rainer suggest beginning with a clearly defined process, choosing one program for each phase, defining each program for a specific aspect of the process, and placing the programs in sequential order.[49]

The process of discipleship does not end with the initial new believer; instead, it moves the believer to become a disciple-maker by encouraging full devotion to Christ and His mission.

This process of spiritual formation must begin with new believers learning to become a disciple since 70 percent of vibrant churches require classes for new members and new believers, but only 38 percent of the comparison churches require these classes.[50] Commenting on the importance of new member courses in reaching the unchurched, Thom Rainer says new member classes lead to a higher retention rate.[51] The church cannot expect new believers to demonstrate good spiritual habits immediately, but they must help them make a commitment to develop habits displayed by the mature in Christ.[52] This basic level of spiritual formation will lead new believers to make commitments to Christ, to spiritual community, to ministry, and to the church and its mission.

The process of discipleship does not end with the initial new believer; instead, it moves the believer to become a disciple-maker by encouraging full devotion to Christ and His mission. Those who become disciples themselves become disciple-makers. In John 15:8, Jesus says, "This is to my Father's glory, that you bear much fruit, showing yourselves to be my disciples." Christ's goal of discipleship is fruitfulness. Spiritual leaders who create new lifecycles will utilize a process that develops the spiritual fruit of Christ's own nature (maturity) and the spiritual fruit of "making disciples" (multiplication). This level of discipleship will help individuals grow in their relationships with Christ, ministry influence, ministry effectiveness, and Kingdom fruitfulness.

Releasing Spiritual Gifts
in the Congregation

Churches that create new lifecycles provide opportunities for believers to receive and give ministry. Spiritual gifts provide the service and ministry of the church. When spiritual gifts operate in the church as intended, they yield edification, growth, and unity in the church (Eph 4:11-16).

Churches that revitalize build a strong infrastructure of ministries that mobilize the laity to fulfill the mission of the church led by a combination of trained staff and lay leadership teams. In *Equipping for Ministry*, John Palmer lists several basic principles that remain biblically foundational in recognizing the role of laity in the church: "all members of the local church are necessary; there is diversity of ministry within the church; there is unity in the church, and members of the church need each other."[53]

Leaders must encourage members to serve, assist them in identifying their gifts, equip them for service, and place them in meaningful ministry. Spiritual leaders carry the responsibility to create a system that equips the body of Christ to serve God by serving one another with their spiritual gifts. To determine one's spiritual gifts, an inventory assessment helps match gifts with the ministry: "While spiritual fruit defines what a Christian is, revealing the character and nature of Christ within the believer (Gal 5:22-23), spiritual gifts determine what a Christian does, revealing the power of Christ working through the believer in service to others (1 Peter 4:10-11)."[54]

One barrier that keeps some churches from growing is an inadequate structure for growth.

Christian Schwarz describes this kind of empowering leadership as a process of motivating and mobilizing the people, providing them opportunities to discover and utilize their unique giftedness and serve in the power of the Holy Spirit[55] Schwarz notes that "when Christians serve in their area of giftedness, they generally function less in their own strength and more in the power of the Holy Spirit. Thus ordinary people can accomplish the extraordinary!"[56] Effective church leaders provide the coaching, mentoring, training, and opportunity to develop the gifting and anointing of the people of God. Wayne Lee sees ministry as both an art and a science: "Spiritual leaders build 'laboratories' for creativity, experimentation, practice, and mistakes."[57]

One barrier that keeps some churches from growing is an inadequate structure for growth. When most of the ministry centers on the pastor, the church's growth potential remains limited to the number of ministry areas the pastor can oversee. A change has to take place in the role of the pastor for churches to grow effectively and reach their full potential, and the people have to step up and use their spiritual gifts.[58] Pastors who create new lifecycles lead their churches to a renewed attitude for service, a passion to serve, and a desire to see the impact of their service. These churches reap the harvest because they have harvest workers. As Joel Comiskey notes, "churches that have no plan to develop leaders have, by default, planned to lose the harvest."[59] Leaders create opportunities for laypeople to release their spiritual gifts.

James R. Clinton provides valuable insight to help leaders discover and develop the gifts of laity.[60] He begins with evaluation, exploration, examination, and experimentation. He offers a four-step process for developing the spiritual gifts: (1) provide new knowledge, (2) model (mentor), (3) offer opportunities for practical use, and (4) provide on-going training.

Ministry is best performed by teams with members
working and communicating together
to reach a common goal.

Ministry is best performed by teams with members working and communicating together to reach a common goal. A team approach allows individuals to use their unique skills and talents, capitalizing on the strengths and spiritual gifts of each person. When team members align their personal goals with the church's missional goals, they release a powerful anointing. Team ministry requires loyalty, commitment, respect, and trust, especially when conflicts and disagreements arise. Effective team ministry will incorporate coaching and mentoring, two-way communication, and ongoing development.

Transformation of the Missional Effectiveness of the Congregation

As part of the Great Commission, evangelism provides the process through which new believers are won to Christ. For a church to fulfill its purpose, it must reach people not actively following Christ and help them start doing so. Creating a new lifecycle requires a renewed commitment to reach and serve the community. This type of outreach remains service-oriented and is frequently called missional service. Serving the community through social action books, working in partnership with local public schools, and other such activities provide the means for reaching the community. McIntosh notes the importance of this outward focus: "When leadership focuses from those already in the church to those in the community, the church is revitalized, and the people in the church experience spiritual growth."[61] The mindset of the congregation shifts from the internal to the external. The church becomes visual and engages the community outside the walls of the church, believing the church exists for this reason. McNeal helps contemporary leaders understand how this shift in thinking redesigns the target of ministry: "Internally focused churches" use their resources on what benefits those already in the church while "externally focused ministry leaders … look for ways to serve the communities where they are located." [62] This shift in focus releases excitement, energy, and life within the church and its people.

Revitalizing pastors help their congregations embrace missional living as a way of life.

35

When this happens, evangelism becomes a process more than an event, and churches embrace incarnational ministry, just as the Early Church did as they were entrenched in their communities. Like the Early Church, the revitalizing church must focus on living, demonstrating, and offering biblical community to a lost world. Stetzer calls this "incarnational living," the way to live the mandate of Christ in one's context of life.[63] Wayne Lee uses the term "Jerusalem Harvest."[64]

> The missional church, however, sees itself as a Kingdom agent deployed in its everyday, natural setting.

In contrast, the traditional church emphasizes reaching people through church outreach efforts and then assimilating them into the church. The missional church, however, sees itself as a Kingdom agent deployed in its everyday, natural setting. McNeal says that "the missional church views the church's position in society as one where God has his people—his missionaries—deployed across all domains of culture. After all, since the mission is redemptive and the world is God's target, does it make sense that he would take this approach?"[65] This shift in philosophy turns members into missionaries, as a "genuine mission impulse is a sending one rather than a fractional one."[66] The church does not merely house the missions program or send missionaries into the world; it exists as the missions program of God: "The existence of the church is the embodiment of Christ's mission."[67] As missionaries study their cultures to be relevant, so does the missional believer work to build bridges for the sake of gaining an opportunity to share the message of salvation.

A missional church evaluates its effectiveness differently
than how most others measure it.

Leaders of missional churches, those creating new lifecycles, acknowledge their responsibility for fulfilling the missionary purpose of the local church. McNeal describes them as "visionaries who are energized by a vision of the preferred future, not just informed by denominational program with the latest methodological book."[68] He describes them as "entrepreneurial," taking calculated risks to create markets for the gospel, and "apostolic" with a genuine spirituality, ones who have the ability to develop "great teams" with the core value of "cultural relevance."[69] Revitalization pastors employ these powerful approaches: they are entrepreneurial, apostolic, spiritual, team-oriented, and culturally relevant.

Pastors of revitalization learn to engage the whole church and lead them in embracing the mandate for evangelism. They remain more intentional in their evangelistic efforts, and they prepare for outreach with prayer and training. For a church to create a new lifecycle, it must regain a passion for evangelism and a passion for the lost.

Transformation of the Management/ Structure of the Congregation

The creation of new lifecycles involves many management and structural realities that include decision-making, finances, facilities, and personnel. Each of these can impact the church's mission. Management systems of the local church aim toward efficiency, giving priority to quality: "The first step in leading a turnaround in an organization is simply to take a good long look at the stark realities— and then to communicate those realities to everyone involved in a way that avoids panic."[70] This involves leadership decisions and management execution. Effective turnaround requires the successful management of tensions and seeks to solve problems.

Revitalizing the church's structure must begin with decision-making.

The local church needs a process of decision-making to ensure sound and wise decisions, manage potential conflicts, and initiate needed change. Rainer and Geiger call for a simple and crystal-clear structure.[71] Leaders that develop such structures will "know their church's process and are able to articulate it to others with conviction. They are able to do so because they own the process."[72] The best process for today's church is both streamlined and participative. In this kind of environment, the church can make quality decisions, which will lead to greater satisfaction among members. It will solve problems before they escalate to a crisis, which prevents disengagement by members. A sound decision-making process also helps in the strategic planning of the church, which is "the process of thinking and acting."[73] The emphasis here should center on enabling leaders to discover and rediscover the God-given mission and strategy.

The best process for today's church is both streamlined and participative.

Without a commitment to embracing biblical values that lead to revitalization and new lifecycles, an unhealthy culture within the church will impede its growth and will fail any strategic plans put into place since "culture eats strategy for lunch."[74] Samuel Chand extensively covers the importance and impact of principles on organizational culture. He believes that culture remains the most important factor in any organization, but it typically goes unnoticed, unspoken, and unexamined; yet it determines how people respond to vision and leadership.[75] At the same time, culture most often surfaces and is addressed through negative experiences. It remains hard to change, but change results in multiplied benefits.[76]

Learning to navigate the terrain of revitalization requires leaders to develop the art of decision-making, which is the skill of flexibility, according to Rutland. He says leaders must be willing to "move and respond according to changing circumstances."[77] This skill is not easily developed and is best accomplished with mentors helping the individual to process the change. Pastors leading change will face resistance from those who desire to protect the status quo, and often these individuals hold the power positions of the church. Wayne Lee has developed a problem-solving process that assists leaders with making decisions. Following his sequential process will help leaders avoid a breakdown in cooperation. The process involves isolating the issue or issues, identifying the participants, gathering and analyzing essential related information, determining possible options, changes, and risks, securing action agreements, and testing, implementing, and communicating the decisions made.[78] This process helps churches that must make many difficult decisions during revitalization.

Pastors leading change will face resistance from those
who desire to protect the status quo

The church, with limited resources, will not be able to continue doing church as it has been doing it. Stetzer's research shows that churches that make a comeback and revitalize often required a change in their facilities to help facilitate the growth, which "included remodeling facilities, building children and youth facilities, but also included marketing."[79] A new building brings excitement and growth to the church. People see the vision for the new building and what the church is trying to accomplish, and they want to be a part of it. However, "build it and they will come" will not bring transformation by itself. Beautiful facilities do not replace an unhealthy culture. While church facilities do not raise the satisfaction level of the church or community, they do tend to lower dissatisfaction.[80] The best guide is to let the vision determine the facilities. As the church catches, embraces, and fulfills the vision, God's resources will follow.

The financial system of the church provides the resources to maintain adequate personnel, ministry programs, and facilities. Lee asserts that "financial resources must convert into the fuel required to maintain the health and growth of the church."[81]

> Pastors creating new lifecycles will need sufficient
> financial resources to stimulate and maintain growth.

The development of good principles and processes will enable the church to properly cultivate and manage financial resources.

Chapter 4

Creating New Lifecycles

Leading a church to create a new lifecycle takes skills and the art of leadership. McIntosh has identified the various leadership styles needed for the different stages of congregational development.[1] They include the following five styles: (1) the Catalyzer, who is needed in the emerging stage of the congregation, has the ability to bring something into being that did not formerly exist; (2) the Organizer, needed in the growing stage of the congregation, has the ability to bring together that which is disorderly because of growth; (3) the Operator, needed in the consolidating stage, has the ability to manage the organization when it is stable; (4) the Reorganizer, needed as the church enters the declining stage, has similar skills as the Organizer but with the added ability to work with a declining church by keeping long-term members happy while building new vision and strategy; and (5) the Super-Reorganizer, needed as a church is in the dying stage, has the ability to bring about radical changes that result in the rebirth of the congregation. These five styles of leadership are crucial at different phases of revitalization and renewal. A style that works at one phase does not always work at a different phase of growth and development. Learning the appropriate styles to use at certain phases encompasses the art of leadership.

Re-Creating Growth Points

For a church to create a new lifecycle, an interruption must occur. A church's current developmental stage determines the level of difficulty that exists in creating momentum and a new lifecycle. McIntosh calls the re-creating point of a lifecycle "choice points."[2] Churches must choose between life and death because at the "point of transition between stages in the life cycle, there is an opportune time for the church to decide to move forward and birth a new cycle of life and vitality or stay on the pathway to plateau and eventual decline and death."[3] During these choices, churches must remain cognizant of the preferred future, which is very difficult when all is going well in the church. Ideally, churches determine "choice points" before decline occurs. It is in these moments that leaders identify new visions, opportunities, and structures for the church: "Churches that have an effective and fruitful ministry for many years actually go through several cycles of birth, growth, and renewal. At each peak of the growth cycle, the church leaders face another choice point."[4] For continuous renewal and growth, it remains critical for leaders to recognize choice points and lead the church to a new growth point, when a congregation experiences "maximum ministry … both inside (spiritual growth) and outside (spiritual birth). Whenever a church finds itself in the balanced position of seeing a significant number of new people coming to faith in Christ and believers already in the church growing in their spiritual lives, it is at its growth point."[5] Pastors that learn to keep the church at its growth point will see the church enjoy its greatest level of joy, excitement, and energy. Returning a church to its growth point is also the point when a new lifecycle begins. The art of leadership consists of walking through this change process.

The Change Process

In the human lifecycle, decline remains inevitable. No matter how much a person exercises, eat healthy food, and visits the doctor, physical decline eventually sets in, leading to death. In organizations, lifecycle decline is not certain, only probable. Organizations of any kind have the potential for renewed growth and vitality. With 70 percent of American churches stagnant or slipping into decline, established churches must find ways to stay focused and effective.[6] While the process remains difficult, some churches can reverse the decline by creating new lifecycles. Values must guide the new lifecycle in creating the program and ministry, fostering behaviors that reflect those values, and cultivating leaders to guide the entire process.

When it comes to creating new lifecycles and leading necessary change, Andy Stanley emphasizes the need to ask the right questions: "Asking the right questions (and asking them over and over) will ensure that the vision of your church remains paramount while your programming remains subservient."[7] Questions that give a clear definition to vision, values, strengths, and weaknesses will help define the needed implementation strategies and systems. The implementation of a change process provides the crucial component needed to bring about a new lifecycle in the church. Michael A. Beitler brings clarity to the process of change: "Change is a process that follows a relatively predictable pattern."[8] Unfortunately, few have experience or training in how to bring about the change process.

Many church growth models utilize components from business and organizational literature, but John Kotter's eight-stage change process serves as a particularly useful classic:

1. Establish a sense of urgency.
2. Create a guiding coalition.
3. Develop vision and strategy for the specific change.
4. Communicate the change vision and strategic plan.
5. Empower employees for action.
6. Generate short-term wins.
7. Consolidate gains and produce more change.
8. Anchor the new changes in the culture.[9]

In addition, one of the more recent church revitalization models comes from Malphurs and Penfold, who encourage pastors to "pursue a process that results in a model."[10] They suggest three stages—the preparation for re-envisioning a church, the process for re-envisioning a church, and the practice of re-envisioning a church.[11] These three stages serve as a guide to leading and developing the processes for organizational change in the local church.

The Preparation for
Re-Envisioning a Church

The first stage of Malphurs's and Penfold's model, the preparation stage, prepares for the re-envisioning process using seven steps (see Table 1). Without preparation, the effort will likely fail.

Table 1: The Preparation for Re-Envisioning a Church

Step 1	Gain Support
Step 2	Draft a Strategic Leadership Team
Step 3	Communicate Constantly
Step 4	Embrace a Theology of Change
Step 5	Conduct a Church Analysis
Step 6	Recruit a Coach or Mentor
Step 7	Lay a Spiritual Foundation

Gaining support and communicating change enables others to adopt the vision and plan. Creating a sense of urgency builds motivation and momentum. Leaders are charged with challenging the status quo. This process remains necessary for re-formation and transitioning God's people to alignment with God's purposes.[12] Kotter's model begins by establishing a sense of urgency: "With urgency low, it's difficult to put together a group with enough power and credibility to guide the effort or to convince key individuals to spend the time necessary to create and communicate a change vision."[13] Without a sense of urgency, people will drift toward complacency without knowing an issue exists. Thus, the downward slope toward death begins. Revitalization begins with leaders confronting a complacent culture with a sense of urgency that calls for a renewed commitment to the mission of Christ. If those in empowered positions do not support the process, change will not occur. The change leader should not proceed forward with the vision until key leaders and others in power give their support; otherwise, much time, energy, and money will go to waste.

Gaining support and communicating change enables others to adopt the vision and plan. Creating a sense of urgency builds motivation and momentum. Leaders are charged with challenging the status quo.

This guiding coalition includes key leaders who know the church and have favor with the congregation: "When congregants know that their leaders are on the team, they recognize the other leaders besides the pastor are a part of the process. This encourages them to be supportive of the team and its work."[14] Kotter recommends pulling together a team that possesses four characteristics: first, they must have position power. It is important that the leader include enough board members and key leaders on the guiding team so progress cannot be easily blocked. Second, leaders must find people with expertise in the various systems of the organization. Third, leaders must build a credible team, so the entire constituency takes seriously the plans and vision. Fourth, the leader must find other proven leaders to help bring about the change process.[15] A guiding coalition remains important.

> The greater the change to the culture of the church, the
> more the team needs people of substantial influence.

Another important step in this stage involves communicating the mission to everyone in the organization. It is easy to falsely assume everyone has bought into the vision. Communication builds trust; without trust, a leader cannot lead. Communicating the vision requires solid statements, metaphors, media, visuals, and slogans. Clear direction is charted through clear communication. This will include both written and spoken communication. The success of implementation depends on clear communication.

The Process for Re-Envisioning a Church

Stage two begins the re-envisioning process. Malphurs and Penfold focus on five biblical core values (worship, fellowship, biblical instruction, evangelism, and service) that enable a church to re-envision itself. They have a four-step process to help a local church define and develop its specific vision and strategy (see Table 2).

Table 2: The Process for Re-Envisioning a Church

Step 1	Develop the Church's Biblical Mission
Step 2	Discover the Church's Core Values
Step 3	Develop the Church's Vision
Step 4	Design the Church's Strategy

This process of re-envisioning is best done in a collaborative environment that includes the pastors, board, staff, and congregation.

In the book, *A Spirit-Empowered Church*, Alton Garrison lays out a process that has proven to be effective in helping a church re-envision itself. He's created assessment tools designed to help churches discover their current condition. These tools will only work if the church leadership has the courage to be honest and then act on their findings.[16]

Every church should be asking the following questions:

1. Why do we exist? (Mission)

2. Where are we going? (Vision)

3. How should we behave? (Values)

4. How will we get there? (Strategic plan)

5. How will we engage new people? (Evangelize/Go)

6. How will we greet them when they arrive? (Connect)

7. How will we disciple them? (Grow)

8. How will we train them to serve? (Serve)

9. How will we inspire them to be missional? (Go)

10. How will we help them encounter God? (Worship)

The Practice of Re-Envisioning
a Church

Stage three involves the practice of re-envisioning a church, which requires evaluation and implementation. This stage consists of five core concepts: "reaching the community, making disciples, building a team, analyzing the setting, and raising the finances."[17] These five concepts enable the church to fulfill its mission.

Kotter describes three steps necessary for the practice of re-envisioning: (1) generate short-term wins, (2) consolidate gains and produce more change, and (3) anchor the new change in the culture.[18] Concerning short-term wins, Rutland notes that "nothing is more important to a turnaround than rolling up small, quick victories that build positive momentum and give everybody the feeling that things are indeed looking up. That change in attitude lays the foundation for bigger victories later on."[19] Leaders cannot ignore this step when attempting to change culture.

Celebrating short-term wins builds credibility throughout
the process.

When celebrating short-term wins, Kotter asserts that the wins must be visible, unambiguous, and clearly relate to the change agent: "The more cynics and resisters, the more important are short-term wins."[20] The key is to generate momentum while bringing about change.

Once leaders make organizational changes, they must make those changes part of the behavioral norms and shared values of the people.[21] Kurt Lewin calls this step "refreezing."[22] Table 3 provides important instructions for anchoring change.[23]

Table 3: Anchoring Change

Anchoring Change	Responses
Come last, not first	Most alterations in norms and shared values come at the end of the change process
Depends on results	New approaches generally sink into culture after it is clear that they work
Requires a lot of talks	Without clear verbal communication and support, people are reluctant to change
May involve turnover	Sometimes, when people are resistant to change, there must be a change in key people
Make decisions on succession crucial	Promotion processes must change to be compatible with the new practices, or the culture will reassert itself

Recreating a lifecycle takes time as one walks through the change process. To see the reality of a turnaround, pastors must repeatedly articulate the vision, encouraging people who oppose change or remain reluctant to change. Resistance can take many forms: attacking, avoiding, complaining, and silence. Since change occurs randomly, not linearly, learning to manage difficulties and make adjustments constitute a necessary part of the implementation process. Revitalization requires constant restructuring to freeze new divine urgencies.

With over 80 percent of churches in plateau or decline, it remains imperative that there exists a vision for church revitalization and a desire to learn the necessary keys to creating new lifecycles of growth that remain essential to survival. Many denominations, including the Assemblies of God, have placed much focus on visionary church planters who can plant spiritually healthy churches, but the Fellowship needs greater focus on the revitalization of established churches. Church renewal can occur at any point in a church's lifecycle; however, "the older a church becomes and the later in the lifecycle renewal is attempted, the more difficult it is to see true resurgence of growth and vitality."[24] Pastors must understand how to keep a church at its growth point for as long as possible or return the church to its growth point. This will enable a new lifecycle to begin, "which can last for another twenty-plus years. However, if a church never returns to its growth point, it will continue with much less vitality, eventually losing so much ministry vigor that it closes its doors or slides into a time of mere survival."[25] Established churches facing decline must reignite their passion and refocus on their purpose. While the process remains difficult, some churches can reverse the decline by creating new lifecycles.

With over 80 percent of churches in plateau or decline, it remains imperative that there exists a vision for church revitalization and a desire to learn the necessary keys to creating new lifecycles of growth that remain essential to survival.

Pastors must realize that any plateau that lasts "for three or more years, are life-threatening, silent killers."[26] Therefore, it remains vital that churches keep vigilant. They must always watch for plateaus and understand the key elements necessary for revitalization. They must become conversant in the process of change that brings about new lifecycles. The Fellowship needs a nationwide movement prompted by the Holy Spirit that leads to revitalized churches fulfilling their mission in their communities for the glory of God, one that powerfully impacts cities and neighborhoods.

Chapter 5

Creating a New Lifecycle in CLC

The Divine Urgency of
Leadership Development

Creating change in an organization requires a guiding coalition. CLC's coalition included the pastoral team, staff, and board of deacons. The coalition worked to build a cohesive team around a common vision. This began with me as the new senior pastor. I needed to build relationships, trust, unity, and vision with the other pastors, ministry staff, board, and lay leaders. I utilized numerous breakfast and lunch appointments, weekly pastor and staff team meetings, monthly board meetings, and regular all church leadership meetings to accomplish this.

Second, the pastors and board members read and studied together several books: *The Speed of Trust, Five Dysfunctions of a Team, The Master Plan of Evangelism, The Advantage,* and *The 360 Degree Leader* and completed numerous video teachings that enabled deeper discussion of how to implement the new vision.

Third, CLC developed a simple and clear vision that embraces the ethnic diversity of the congregation and motivates the church to fulfill its mission. With Wayne and Sherry Lee, we held a vision retreat for two days with all pastors, board, and spouses. Topics included the layering of Pentecostalism, church life model, transformational bridge graphic, team formation, personality types, vision, values assessment, and conflict resolution. The retreat led us to develop our mission and vision with a simple visual graphic.

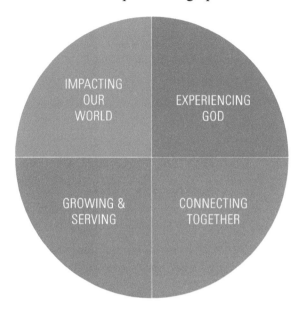

The retreat also outlined a mission statement that continued to be developed with the pastoral staff over a period of four to six weeks, which ultimately became "Experiencing God, Connecting Together, Growing and Serving, and Impacting Our World." A prayer was also written that was used to conclude worship services each week: "Father, help us to be the people and the church you have called us to be. A people that always build up, and never tear down, who always encourage and never discourage. A people and a church who take a message of hope everywhere we go, to everyone we meet. In Jesus's name, Amen." We developed a short personal mission slogan too: "messengers of hope." Logos, bulletins, the website, social media, video announcements, and all print materials began reflecting the new vision.

Fourth, we determined that there were not enough leaders for the current size or next level of the church. When arriving to CLC, we had approximately seventy-five leaders for a church that was averaging around 1,750 each weekend. To advance to our next level of 2500, we needed to develop an additional 175 leaders serving in ministry. To address this problem, a leadership development pipeline was put into place that would include a spiritual retreat, a discipleship process, and leadership coaching.

The Divine Urgency of
Spiritual Life

CLC's spiritual life needed stronger emphasis to lift the church's spiritual passion in several areas. CLC needed individuals to renew their personal relationship with the Lord, especially in the area of private devotions. Church leaders also felt that the church needed greater emphasis on the presence of God and freedom of the Spirit during weekend services. Services had grown too restrictive and structured, with little flexibility for a move of the Holy Spirit. Few opportunities existed for congregants to experience the presence or gifts of the Spirit, and few were being baptized in the Spirit.

In response to these issues, we designed the Encounter Retreat, a three-day weekend spiritual retreat held at a local retreat center to give extended times for prayer and the seeking of the Holy Spirit. We scheduled revival and renewal nights and invited speakers gifted with seeking the Holy Spirit and altar calls. We held prayer vigils several times a year, two of which were all-night services with close to seven hundred in attendance. In addition, my wife, Candi, took the role of pastor of spiritual life to oversee Encounter Retreat and the new prayer ministries Healing Point and Gate Keepers.

CLC's spiritual life also lacked core prayer meetings. In response, my pastoral team, ministry staff, and I began incorporating thirty minutes of prayer in our weekly staff meetings. We also changed the format of Wednesday evening services to include times of intense prayer. These prayer times focused on remaining prophetic, God-centered, and learning to discern God's agenda for His people.

During the pandemic, corporate prayer was able to increase as a new method was implemented. Platforms such as Zoom, WhatsApp, and other programs enabled members to connect regularly for passionate prayer without the time demands of travel. This has become a powerful tool for increasing corporate prayer.

CLC needed individuals to renew their personal
relationship with the Lord.

CLC also began to change the worship services to include more margin in service programming to facilitate supernatural moments for the release of God's grace. This led to having regular nights and seasons for spiritual renewal. We call these nights, *Nights Ablaze*, with extended time for worship; revivalists as guest speakers invited to minister; and times of seeking, soaking, and laying on of hands in the altars—believing for a supernatural move of God.

Finally, we chose a theme for each year: i.e., *imagine more*, *breakthrough*, etc. The theme features a twenty-one-day prayer and fasting focus, including four weeks of devotional guides to accompany a sermon series on the state of the church. During the year-long theme, we continue to believe that God will weave that theme into the fabric of the life of the church and believers.

The Divine Urgency of
Spiritual Community

One area that was a deficit and needed urgent change was authentic relational connections. When I first came to CLC, the church offered twenty-three life groups, small groups of ten to twenty congregants who met in various homes. Nearly everyone to whom I spoke was starved for friendship and relationships. In response, we decided to multiply life groups, but we needed to train new leaders for these groups. As a result, we developed the School of Discipleship to train group leaders, which eventually enabled us to add sixty-four more groups for a total of eighty-seven groups. As of October 2022, CLC has 140 small groups, 250 leaders helping to lead these groups, and close to 1700 participants.

A major area of development needed at CLC was the assimilation process, helping newcomers get connected to the local church. This vital function "is the process of connecting a person or family to the local church; it involves incorporating new people into the life of the local assembly.

The assimilation process helps the church to preserve the fruits gained from evangelism."[1]

Wayne Lee

To strengthen this system, CLC implemented several changes. First, we hired a new staff pastor to oversee assimilation and ministry connection. This pastor developed an assimilation strategy and formed the Red Carpet Team, which recruited and trained volunteers, implemented a new software system, Church Community Builder, to track and contact large numbers of new congregants, and put more intentional focus on connection.

We implemented new systems for visitors, new converts, membership, and baptisms. The assimilation system was designed to "start the minute someone drives into the parking lot, steps foot in the church, or before."[2]

Improving authentic relational connection meant we also needed to strengthen congregant care, or biblical shepherding, within the church. This included improving comfort, prayer, encouragement, and ministering to special needs that arise. To meet the vast number of needs in our large church, we gave specialized training to life group leaders, so they could better meet the needs of their group members. We also created a ministry called *Healing Point*, which gives a specialized and intentional prayer for those in physical, emotional, financial, or spiritual difficulty.

The Divine Urgency of Discipleship/Ministry

Though we had discipleship classes, they lacked systematic spiritual, ministry, and leadership formation. No path existed to help direct new believers in their spiritual growth, to help members identify and engage in ministry service, or to provide formal leadership development. As a result, we focused on strategically implementing a discipleship and leadership process. We identified simple steps for developing spiritual growth in new guests, new believers, and regular attendees, illustrated in a simple graphic.

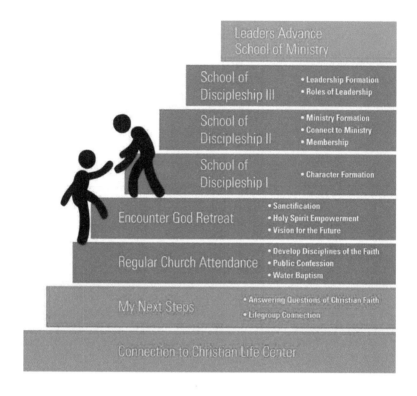

This led to the development of new courses to accomplish the missional values for each group, which included Starting Point, Alpha, Encounter Retreat, and School of Discipleship (SOD). As we implemented each of the divine urgencies, the Encounter Retreats and SOD began to shift the mindset and culture of CLC, which helped the church embrace its missional values and create a new lifecycle.

The Encounter Retreat

A key to the transformational process implemented at CLC is the Encounter Retreats. The retreat provides a spiritual outing with God, in which one fully experiences His presence and is based on this biblical principle: a time of separation and of dying to self during a period of three days, as set forth in Hosea 6:1-3. The retreat provides a time when a believer leaves behind family, work, and worries in order to fully concentrate on God. It begins on a Thursday evening and ends on a Saturday afternoon. CLC leaders encourage everyone, not just new believers, to attend a retreat since even mature believers may have unresolved issues that need addressing. Encounter Retreat also caters to those desiring a deeper level of intimacy with the Lord. CLC leaders emphasize that this retreat should result in a time that the believer will always cherish and remember as an encounter with Jesus.

The three-day retreat deals with five themes: the Father's love, sanctification, the work of Christ on the Cross, Holy Spirit baptism, and vision. The retreat is designed to lead to a total transformation, one that gives birth to the character of Christ in the believer. Topics covered during the retreat may also include rejection, spiritual pride, sexual sins, repentance, the sanctification of unconfessed sin, inner healing, and/or deliverance from demonic oppression.

On the last day of the retreat, a significant amount of time focuses on the work of the Holy Spirit and His power.

The retreat provides a spiritual outing with God, in which one fully experiences His presence and is based on this biblical principle: a time of separation and of dying to self during a period of three days, as set forth in Hosea 6:1-3.

During the retreat, spiritual sensitivity improves in participants, greatly enhancing their ability to hear God. It is also one of the primary ways that CLC enables its members to experience the baptism of the Holy Spirit. The ultimate goal of Encounter Retreat is for participants to receive a greater vision for the harvest so that they clearly understand and receive the mandate of Christ "to go and make disciples" and God's vision for the Church.

Changes Due to Pandemic Encounters

At the beginning of the COVID-19 Pandemic, Encounters moved from off-site at hotels or retreat center facilities to being on-campus at CLC. Participants commute from home, which reduces the risk of the spread of COVID-19, and also reduces the cost of lodging. Though it is more challenging for the participants, CLC has found that this enabled us to continue to conduct 4-5 Encounters a year. To ensure punctuality at the start of each day, prayer team leaders contact their participants in the morning to ensure their attendance and encourage the importance of beginning on time. All meals are provided at the church, including breakfast.

CLC encourages members to attend an Encounter before starting School of Discipleship. However, during the pandemic, this requirement was loosened since many were uncomfortable being in large gatherings, in close proximity to others, or were a part of CLC's online family in other cities, states, and nations. For those that did start SOD before going to an Encounter, they were required to attend an Encounter before their SOD Graduation.

CLC has been partnering with national movements of several countries to help hold Encounter for their pastors and ministers. These pastors learn how to conduct an Encounter weekend with the purpose of implementing it within their local church context. Several pastors in a geographical area often will link together to hold Encounters to help with the weight of running the weekend.

From an Encounter Retreat, participants are encouraged to continue into School of Discipleship (SOD).

School of Discipleship

SOD provides the opportunity to renew the mind. There, believers grow in their relationship with God, discover and embrace their ministries to the Body, and grow in leadership principles. SOD is carefully developed to address the crucial components of spiritual formation, ministry skills and gifts development, leadership skills and execution, and growth through mentorship by other leaders.

SOD consists of three levels; each level consists of ten weeks of training with two lessons per week. Therefore, SOD provides sixty lessons given over a nine-month period.

Before SOD, new believers are led to take a basics to the faith class, *Next Steps*. This has been developed into a small booklet that deals with six of the most vital steps for a new believer: Prayer, Bible Study, Small Group Connection, Baptism, and Sharing of one's faith. This book has also been produced in an e-book and pdf format so that we can easily send it electronically.

Once an individual makes a commitment to faith, they are asked to let us know by texting "decision" to a number that then activates a follow-up system. This system includes a short three- to five-minute video of the topic of the week in the *Next Steps* book. Individuals are then invited to an in-person and virtual discussion time of each chapter. The goal of this time is to answer questions they may have in their new walk with the Lord, as well as connecting them with small group leaders.

This process is connected to an outdoor water baptism and celebration of their commitment to Christ. They are encouraged to invite their friends and family and to share a testimony of their newfound faith in Christ.

As one is taking these initial steps in their walk with the Lord, there is typically an Encounter God Retreat where they are encouraged to take the next step and attend the Encounter.

At the School of Discipleship (SOD), believers grow in their relationship with God, discover and embrace their ministries to the Body, and grow in leadership principles.

From the Encounter, the following week, a new SOD is beginning. All are encouraged to continue to take the next step in their spiritual growth.

In the chart below, you will see the scope and sequence of the topics taught in the Alpha Course and all three levels of the School of Discipleship. The Alpha Course has been recently replaced with the Next Steps process, but the topics are similar.

Week	Hour	Growth In Christ	Growth In Spiritual Formation	Growth In Ministry Formation	Growth In Leadership Formation
		ALPHA	SOD 1	SOD 2	SOD 3
1	Hr. 1	Is there more to life than this?	Your Character and Truth	Power of a Vision	Law of the Lid
	Hr. 2	Who is Jesus?	Seizing the Opportunity	The Heart of Ministry	Morning Matters
2	Hr. 1	Why did Jesus die?	Men: A Man and His God Women: Purpose of Life	The Necessity of Spiritual Community	What is a Leader?
	Hr. 2	How Can We Have Faith?	Men: Men in the Bible Women: God Values Women	Unwrapping the Gifts Pt 1	Stucture of a Lifegroup
3	Hr. 1	Why and How do I pray?	Salvation and Repentance	Unwrapping the Gifts Pt 2	Leadership is Influence
	Hr. 2	What and How should I read the bible?	Men: A Man and his Relationships with Other Men Women: Developing your Character	Unwrapping the Gifts Pt 3	Relationship Between Group Leaders and Members
4	Hr. 1	How does God Guide us?	The New Birth	S.H.A.P.E	Requirements for Successful Leadership
	Hr. 2	Who is the Holy Spirit?	Men: A Man of Purity Women: Growing to Your Fullness	Connection to Ministry	Handeling Conflict
5	Hr. 1	What does the Holy Spirit do?	Surrender and Lordship	The Ways of Evangelism	How to Teach for Real Results
	Hr. 2	How can I be filled with the Holy Spirit?	Men: Battle plan of Sexual Purity Women: A look at Sexual Integrity	Breaking Intimidation	Qualities of Potential Leaders
6	Hr. 1	How can I make the most of the rest of my life?	The bible	Share your Testimony Pt. 1	Dangers of Leadership
	Hr. 2	How can I resist Evil?	M: A Man and His children W:The Family on God's Heart	Bait of Satan:Bait of Offense	A Person of Influence has Faith in People
7	Hr. 1	Why and How should I tell others?	Prayer	Share your Testimony Pt. 2	Developing your Annointing
	Hr. 2	Does God Heal today?	Men: A Man and His Mentors Women: Developing Relationships	Understanding the Needs of New Believers	Alter Worker Training
8	Hr. 1	What about the Church?	Faith	Power of Assimilation	Faith Goals
	Hr. 2		Men: A Man and his Church Women: Preparing for Excellence	Undercover: Kicking Against the Goads	Counseling and Ministering to the Needs of others
9	Hr. 1		Holy Spirit	Spiritual Warfare	SOD Reflection
	Hr. 2		The Necessity of Spiritual Community	Undercover: Obedience & Submission	The Heart of Leadership
10	Hr. 1		Overcoming Obstacles	The Master Plan of Evangelism	What's Next?
	Hr. 2		Final Exam	Bait of Satan: My Father, My Father	Celebration
11	Hr. 1		Community Life		
	Hr. 2				

64

Level one addressed spiritual formation (being), level two concerned ministry formation (doing), and level three encompassed leadership formation (leading others). Each week had action steps for application along with homework. Participants turned in their weekly work, which a team of volunteers then graded.

A team of mentors worked with each group of participants as they went through all three levels in small groups called "cadres." A cadre is defined as "a small group of people specially trained for a particular purpose." These mentors are called "Cadre Leaders" and their primary role was to encourage participants and keep them engaged through the entire process.

Level One: Spiritual Formation

Level one built on the foundations established in the Alpha course and the renewed passion from the Encounter Retreat. The teaching was divided into two one-hour sessions. The first hour, called doctrine, focused on being what Christ has called believers to be: transformed into His image. We emphasized character formation and reinforced that with homework and Scripture memorization. Students read through the New Testament during the ten weeks. The second hour, known as seminar, highlighted the importance of becoming men and women of God. Women and men are separated for these sessions. This level also emphasized connection to a life group, which was a requirement for proceeding to level two: ministry formation.

Level Two: Ministry Formation

Level two equipped students to learn how to do what Christ has commissioned them to do: win souls and make disciples. The course focused on discovering one's spiritual gifts, ministry connection, and developing one's story (testimony). Video teaching covered several topics, such as overcoming offense, coming under spiritual authority, spiritual warfare, and breaking intimidation. Students stay together for both hours of teaching in levels two and three. The second hour introduces the mission, vision, strategy, assimilation process, and the need for a spiritual community. Connection to a ministry is a requirement before proceeding to level three: leadership formation.

Level Three: Leadership Formation

Level three enables the student to learn effective leadership as one who understands and develops their anointing and influence for Kingdom impact. It also teaches the student how to become a disciple-maker. Lessons inspire students toward fruitfulness in ministry and include handling conflict, teaching, dangers of leadership, ministry at the altars, counseling, and multiplying one's life group. Level three helps one become a better leader and disciple-maker in the work of building the kingdom of God.

Changes Due to Pandemic

The pandemic also affected SOD. The program moved to a digital platform, and pastors and teachers would teach through the Zoom platform. Each lesson was also recorded by the pastors/teachers so that when they were unavailable, the video could also be shown.

A few years into the pandemic, it was felt that an online digital platform, though convenient, lacked some relational connection between students with each other and with the pastors/teachers. Currently, CLC does a hybrid of both online and in-person classes.

The Divine Urgency of
the Jerusalem Harvest

In the first year of creating a new lifecycle for CLC, the church needed to determine its Jerusalem Harvest. A lack of understanding existed about the differences among evangelism, home missions, and outreach. CLC directed outward ministry to the inner city, prisons, and homeless; however, the church's vision needed to expand to impact all segments of society. This would require a paradigm shift.

The initial survey revealed demographics that CLC needed to consider for felt need ministries: women comprise 69 percent of congregants, and singles represent 47 percent of the church, 54 percent of whom have children living at home (single parents). The survey also showed that ethnic minorities comprise 91 percent of CLC, with most identifying as Caribbean, Latino, and Portuguese. To reach and connect these ethnicities, we started relational evangelistic evenings called Christ in Culture, which grouped together congregants with shared ethnic backgrounds. The culturally and linguistically relevant evenings took place once a quarter. At the time of launching these events, we did not envision what would eventually lead to Peter Wagner's Multi-Congregation Model.[3] However, the change provided the seed for our current multi-campus strategy as the Spanish congregation sprang forth from Christ in Culture.

It was immediately discovered through assessments and dialog with pastors, staff, and board that the bussing ministry from the inner city had become a major issue in the church. Over the past several years, many of the congregants have become uncomfortable with the increasing inner-city environment of the kids and youth ministry. Teens bussed in from the inner city reached numbers of eighty to 100 kids, while church teens only numbered fifty to sixty. CLC leaders had to process this very sensitive issue with great care. We needed to focus on the vision to disciple the teens and not just gather large crowds for services. We emphasized the responsibilities of the outreach department for this ministry, not just the youth and children's ministries.

As a result, we moved the outreach bussing ministry to Tuesday evenings and recruited new leaders and volunteers to work with this program. During the pandemic, this ministry was paused and has taken on a different format following the pandemic, in that, now we go into the community and have weekly services in the neighborhoods and help provide transportation on Sundays to services.

A major focus of growth over the past ten years has been the development of a communication or public relations department to share information with both the congregation and the community. Both need to receive communication: "The internal audience builds a spiritual, relational community for others to join. The external audience consists of the potential constituents, the church of the future."[4] Through the pandemic, this area of church ministry has grown substantially, as all aspects of ministry are now phygital (Physical & Digital). We have learned that with this area comes increased impact and increased financial cost.

The Divine Urgency of Management

CLC has wonderful facilities, and through the years, we have continued to (1) add "wow" to the children's' facilities, (2) remodel lobby, colors, and audio/visional, (3) relocate the bookstore and create a welcome center/café, (4) remodel the youth auditorium, (5) remodel the fellowship hall (6) and add "pop" to the outside of the facility to improve curb appeal with new signage and landscaping, and (7) increase parking capacity.

Annually, CLC has a vision campaign called *Heart for The House*, where projects as presented that will enable the church to upgrade and expands its ministries.

Practical Results

The practical results of this book involved creating a new lifecycle for CLC by leading change in six missional values or divine urgencies through a paradigm shift. In response, CLC developed a transformational process to impact pastors, board, leaders, and congregants. The implementation of this new lifecycle allowed CLC to see significant growth spiritually, financially, relationally, and numerically.

The process contributed to ministry growth in several ways: it (1) increased spiritual health, (2) increased relational connections, (3) increased volunteerism, (4) increased leaders, (5) increased numerical growth, and (6) increased financial health.

The last part of this book will prove beneficial to other churches and pastors who need vital information and principles for creating a new lifecycle within their own contexts.

Pentecostal churches must fulfill the mandate and mission of Christ. In order to do so, however, they need to be healthy. They need to embrace God's vision for their community, discover His divine urgencies for their churches, design intentional systems and processes that break restricting behaviors, and cultivate a giving ministry that fulfills God's purposes and develops leaders and members who remain passionately committed to Kingdom values. The remainder of the book will demonstrate that churches can indeed renew themselves to further His mission.

Chapter 6

The Process of Making Disciples

This chapter begins by laying the groundwork for CLC's discipleship process and explaining the importance of engaging in the process. It starts with CLC's **mission**—defining our purpose. This is followed by step-by-step explanations of the **vision**—the direction we're taking to carry out our purpose that will allow us to achieve the objectives God has given us.

Building on these foundations is essential to growth by defining our role individually and within the church. The chapter reviews what a disciple *is*, understanding discipleship as the key to spiritual growth, and the phases of discipleship. It's important to know where one's at in the process to move forward.

Following chapter 6's overview, chapters 7-10 individually address each aspect of *how* a believer first becomes a disciple and then grows to become a disciple-maker—through the process of sharing, connecting, training, and releasing.

Understanding Our Mission

CLC'S mission is to serve as MESSENGERS OF HOPE.

That's what we're here to do. This purpose is important to understand the *why* of discipleship.

Jesus commissioned His disciples with the mission of serving as His messengers in the last chapter of Matthew's Gospel:

Then Jesus came to them and said, "All authority in heaven and on earth has been given to me. Therefore go and make disciples of all nations, baptizing them in the name of the Father and of the Son and of the Holy Spirit, and teaching them to obey everything I have commanded you. And surely I am with you always, to the very end of the age" (Matt 28:18-20, NIV).

In contemporary literature, mission statements vary and can often be confused with vision statements. For CLC, our mission statement is a short statement as to why we exist and our overall goal. As Messengers of Hope, we are a lighthouse of hope to those in need of spiritual and physical care. We are a people and a church that take a message of Hope everywhere we go to everyone we meet.

Understanding Our Vision

To accomplish the mission, we need to grab hold of the plan laid out of how to get there – the vision. Some refer to the vision as the purpose.

The vision of CLC is to:

(1) experience God,

(2) connect together,

(3) grow in Christ by serving Him, and

(4) impact our world.

The graph on the following page shows this vision. Everything we do moves us through these four areas.

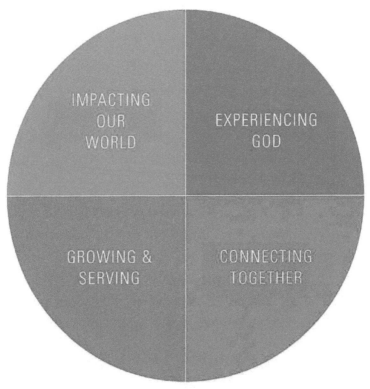

As we grow and walk out the vision, it allows us to multiply the kingdom of God by fulfilling the Great Commission of Jesus to make disciples. First, however, one must be a disciple. Let's define what a disciple is.

Understanding What a Disciple *Is*

A disciple is "a pupil or follower of a teacher or school" according to Webster's Dictionary. A disciple in the Bible refers to someone who follows Christ. This begins with experiencing God and choosing to follow Christ. This may sound easy, but it will require faith and obedience, and a willingness to do things God's way.

A biblical example of this is the rich young ruler who had all the wealth one could ask for. He came to Jesus and asked him what he must do to inherit eternal life. They discussed the law – the dos and don'ts – which he grew up under and knew very well. Even so, the young man wrestled with the idea that there was still more. Jesus then said, "You still lack one thing. Sell everything you have and give to the poor, and you will have treasure in heaven. Then come, follow me" (Luke 18:22, NIV). The young ruler was sad because he had to choose between being wealthy and successful in the eyes of man or giving up all that he knew and was comfortable with God.

Following Jesus and being His disciple means committing to a process of growth that will transform a person individually while allowing people to grow together and serve others. Most importantly, it empowers one to glorify God and walk out His purposes.

A true disciple takes this meaning to the next level by being a follower who applies what he or she has learned.

A true follower of Jesus will believe what He says, walk out His commands, and reflect His image.

Their will begins to align with His will. This takes place through total surrender. Jesus says it best: "If anyone would come after me, let him deny himself and take up his cross and follow me" (Matt 16:24, ESV).

A Disciple Knows and
Follows Christ

When Jesus walked the earth, he had twelve men who became his main disciples. The first pair he called as he was walking along the sea of Galilee – Simon Peter and his brother Andrew. "Come, follow me," Jesus said, "and I will send you out to fish for people" (Matt 4:19, NIV). By leaving their job fishing for fish and following Jesus, they placed themselves under the authority of Jesus and would come to grow in knowledge and truth of who Jesus is. It involved a commitment to spend time with Him and experience a spiritual process of growing through the stages of development, much like the physical process of life: baby/child, young adult to parent.

In Luke 9, Jesus says to his disciples, "If anyone would come after me, let him deny himself and take up his cross daily and follow Me" (Luke 9:23, NIV). Being His disciple is a choice one makes every day where one commits to learn, hear and apply God's Word.

This begins with a transition of the mind—intentionally deciding to leave everything else behind. The disciples followed him from place to place, committed to giving up the things they were comfortable with and their own desires in order to make themselves completely available to His mission. Luke tells us, "For what does it profit a man if he gains the whole world and loses or forfeits himself? (Luke 9:25, ESV). Had their focus been on material things and success through human understanding, they would actually lose it. Jesus's disciples were not to be ashamed of Him or His words but to boldly proclaim the message of salvation and restoring the original relationship to God as it was intended so that one day, Jesus would

75

not be ashamed of them before His Father (v. 26). The same holds true for Jesus's disciples today.

A Disciple is Being
Changed by Christ

As we follow Christ and grow spiritually, we strive to become more like Him in our thoughts, actions, and behavior. We begin to see a transformation from the inside out. We continue to grow as we learn to use the resources God has already provided for us – the Bible, prayer, shared experiences, and the wisdom and knowledge of those who have gone before us (disciple-makers).

The Apostle Paul writes how this transformative process takes place because the disciple's *mind* is, and continues to be, renewed on a regular basis (Rom 12:2). As a result, the disciple begins to show the fruit of the Spirit (Gal 5:22) in dealing with both individual circumstances and in how they treat others. This reflects the nature of God and serves as a testimony to others who don't know Christ and what it looks like to be a disciple of Christ.

As we grow in our relationship with Jesus, others begin to recognize the change in us from needing a Savior to someone who has spent time with Jesus. It is during this time we learn to reflect the glory of God, share Him with others and begin to fulfill the calling He's given us. We become world changers.

A Disciple is Committed
to the Mission of Christ

Part of a disciple's focus is carrying out Christ's mission. As we grow in our relationship with Christ, we begin to see the world and the people in it differently. The more time we spend with Jesus, we begin to recognize new ways to be his hands and feet. We want to serve God wherever He has placed us. This means allowing God to use our abilities, gifts, and skills for the Lord's mission to reconcile people to God (2 Cor 5:20), so that they may become disciples.

At CLC, joining Christ on His mission is an important aspect of the discipleship process. Believers are empowered by the Holy Spirit to fulfill the mission Christ has given us. Mike Clarensau says, "the Spirit-empowered life is focused outward, not just in serving but in spreading the gospel message."[1] Living a missional lifestyle is something that has to be constantly emphasized, giving training and providing opportunities.

As we continue to mature spiritually, the transformation within us begins to overflow, and the result is bearing spiritual fruit, which Jesus Himself says glorifies God and is a sign of being His disciple (John 15:8). At this point, the discipleship process can be reproduced, and the Great Commission of going into the world and making disciples of all nations continues to be fulfilled (Matt 28:18-20).

As a disciple goes through the process of knowing and following Christ, is changed by Him, and becomes committed to His mission, it is important to recognize what stage one is at as a disciple. Once you are a disciple committed to helping make *other* disciples, it is vital to understand the nature of this process in terms of how disciples are growing spiritually.

Understanding Discipleship as
the Key to Spiritual Growth

The Bible is all about relationship. Matthew 22:37-40 sums up how we are to live in two commands: Love God and love others. Jesus modeled this process in His Words and actions. He has called us to do the same. As we continue to grow spiritually and learn to live out our calling, we teach and serve others so that they may begin to do the same. Once they grow through the stages and develop their understanding of how to live as Jesus did, they can help others grow. The following graph, along with the rest of the book, explains the specific stages of spiritual growth in the discipleship process. Ask yourself where you and those you may be discipling are at in the cycle. These answers are important so each person can move closer to the next stage.

Phases of Discipleship

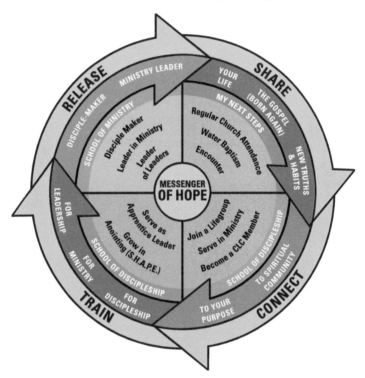

The process of discipling others requires keeping three key principles in mind:

1. **Be an intentional leader**; Jesus intentionally met people where they were at spiritually. Ask questions and listen to find out where people are at as you begin to lead them through the discipleship process.

2. **Establish an atmosphere for building relationships**; Jesus spent three years with His disciples doing life together. Create ways to build environments that allow you to get to know others, have fun, and share experiences together. This

will help build new friends you can trust and be accountable to.

3. **Utilize a reproducible process**; Jesus spent three years training and preparing the disciples to make disciples. While He was still with them, He sent them out two by two, giving them the authority to tell everyone to repent of their sins and turn to God. He instilled in them how to teach others all he had taught them.

As the arrow in the graphic above shows, discipleship is not a linear process that finishes once you've gone through the cycle but a reproducible process that helps guide people in what they need to know to live out God's purpose and how to do it. As a mature Christian who have walked through the discipleship process, now they can intentionally become disciple-makers, leading others through the stages of spiritual growth.

For the purpose of teaching, we will present the circle graphic in a linear format to help grasp the concepts; however, both graphics represent the same process, a transformational process of discipleship.

The following chapter examines the first phase in the discipleship process: *Sharing*.

Chapter 7

Making Disciples: SHARE

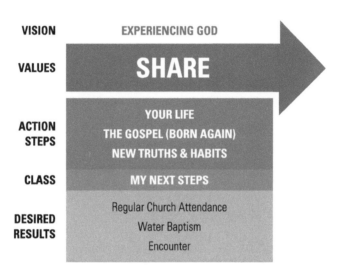

To experience God, one needs to come to see their need for God. Some realize their need and are just waiting to be invited to church. Others have never heard about God or haven't made the decision to believe in Him. They are spiritually dead or spiritual infants.

A biblical example of this is in Hebrews 3:14-19, where the author writes about those among the Israelites who rebelled and did not believe:

> We have come to share in Christ, if indeed we hold our original conviction firmly to the very end. As it has just been said: "Today, if you hear his voice, do not harden your hearts

as you did in the rebellion." Who were they who heard and rebelled? Were they not all those Moses led out of Egypt? And with whom was he angry for forty years? Was it not with those who sinned, whose bodies perished in the wilderness? And to whom did God swear that they would never enter his rest if not to those who disobeyed? So we see that they were not able to enter, because of their unbelief.

For those who are spiritually dead, an encounter with God introduces them to a lifestyle of learning about God through His Word and relationships with others. This is the beginning stage of discipleship. A disciple-maker will begin this process by Sharing — building relationships that can open doors for sharing the gospel. This can be done with friends, neighbors and through community outreach and events. As the graphic above shows, disciple-makers share their lives, the gospel (good news about Jesus) and then help new disciples understand new truths and develop new habits for spiritual growth. This process involves answering important questions regarding faith and God and by sharing your story.

Sharing Your Life

When a spiritually dead person receives Christ, he or she is like an infant that needs to be nurtured and grow naturally into childhood. An infant takes a lot of time and effort on the part of the parents/caregiver. We don't expect a baby to take care of itself; the parent bathes, dresses, feeds, and makes sure all the needs are met.

In the same way that a baby does not know what to do or how to act, spiritual infants need to be fed and cared for. This occurs when a more mature believer shares their life with the spiritual infant.

As Christians, we need to share our lives with others, especially those we are discipling, which includes doing things together, such as: having meals, going to special events, and having fun hanging out with each other. All these things require a commitment to spend time together.

Sharing the Gospel Message

A spiritual infant generally has no idea what it looks like to be a Christian. They need to be introduced to God's Word and discover how God speaks through His Word. The Word of God is active and gives everyone all the answers they're searching for. They need to learn to recognize God's voice and learn to listen to Him. With the help of a spiritual parent, they can learn how to experience Scripture by putting it into practice.

When sharing new truth, the spiritual parent must begin by listening in order to assess how much a person already knows.

Young disciples frequently have common questions that can easily be answered, so it is important for a spiritual parent, also known as a disciple-maker, to be available to answer questions and respond to such teachable moments.

The disciple-maker also needs to continue to have fresh encounters with God. People need to not be so busy ministering and serving that they forget to soak in the presence of God. We can teach others to recognize God's voice and listen by modeling it. As it says: "But be doers of the word, and not hearers only, deceiving yourselves" (Jas 1:22, ESV).

As doers, we also need to live out what God's Word says, not just read and memorize it. One way to do this is by activating the principles of scripture in the life of another person. This goes back to building relationships with others so they can learn to follow God as they follow you.

Jesus exemplified this while on Earth. Though thousands of people followed him from place to place, he consistently withdrew from the crowds, first to spend time in His Father's presence and then to focus on the Twelve. During this time, he continued to teach them and share deeper truths with them. He made himself available to answer questions.

Sharing New Truth/New Habits

As a new believer, they need to grow to the next level: a child. It is the job of a spiritual parent to help them develop by teaching them how to connect with God in a personal way. This will allow spiritual infants to learn how to connect with God in a way that will lead them to abide in Christ and have a solid connection to God where they can continue to grow in their personal relationship with Him.

The spiritual parent can begin this process of development with the spiritual infant by sharing new truths and setting up new habits with them. The first habit that the spiritual infant can begin with is Bible reading. Disciple-makers can share this habit by setting up a regularly scheduled time to read and discuss scripture passages, whether by topic or a chapter of a book, with the new believer.

Many people begin by reading the New Testament, such as the book of John. As they read more and begin to understand the Bible better, they will be encouraged to read it on their own.

CLC recommends the S.O.A.P. method of Bible Study. This is an acrostic that stands for:

S – Scripture – We recommend a systematic approach to Bible Reading. For example, reading one book at a time or through the New Testament.

O – Observation – What is God saying to you? What do you see? What was the author telling his audience? What is the passage about? If there are any words that stand out, look them up, study them, and use another reference to get an overview of the passage.

A – Application – How do you apply this truth/passage to your life? Are there any areas in your life that do not align with the scripture where you need to make changes?

P – Prayer – Take some time to pray about what God has revealed to you in this time through His Word, your observations, and the application for your life. Ask the Lord how you can implement this verse in your life.

Remember, the spiritual infant
must be guided in what to do.

As a Christian matures, Bible reading will give way to more in-depth study, and the disciple-maker can begin to introduce tools and methods for Bible study. Remember, the spiritual infant must be guided in what to do. Teach them how to journal about what they learn, write out prayers, and highlight things that are meaningful or important in their Bibles.

Another habit to teach the new believer is how to share the gospel. They have good news to share with their family and friends, as well as neighbors, co-workers, and acquaintances who have not yet heard! Encourage them to simply tell their story to others of how they came to Christ. Show them by sharing your story. Tell your disciple how you came to Christ—where you were in life before you put your faith in Him, repented of your sins, and committed to a life of obedience to God.

As you share new truths and habits with the new believer, also encourage them to get into the habit of praying. Spiritual infants need to learn to pray, and the best way for this to happen is to combine telling and showing them how to do it. Teaching about prayer is important, but practicing prayer is a more effective way for them to learn. Infants can start by simply praying with you. Walk them through the different types of prayer and show them examples throughout the Scriptures. Help them identify and write a list of people to pray for who need to know Jesus.

A very important step for new believers is to develop the habit of regular church attendance and getting connected to a small group.

Regular church attendance gives believers the opportunity to know (consider) each other in order to promote (spur) one another on to "love and good deeds" (Heb 10:24). Regular attendance in church and in a small group encourages the new believer throughout the week. The Apostle Peter understood the metaphor of new believers being like newborn babies who "crave pure spiritual milk so that you will grow into a full experience of salvation" (1 Pet 2:2, NLT). Just like a baby tastes milk and wants more because of how good it is, a spiritual baby will "Cry out for this nourishment, now that you have had a taste of the Lord's kindness" (v. 3, NLT).

My Next Steps Class

Once one has come to Christ, the discipleship process begins. At CLC, we guide them in their spiritual journey to learning and discovering the basics of faith in a class called My Next Steps. This is the step in which we'll help the new believer answer questions they have about the Christian faith, as well as guide them through a process of connecting with others in a small group. This class helps them discover several keys to walking in Christ as a new believer. The new believer learns the values of prayer, bible study, sharing their new faith in Christ, small group connection, serving in ministry, and water baptism.

Desired Results

Sharing phase leads the new believer to begin to regularly attend worship services where they can experience God, build community, grow in faith, learn to serve Christ by serving His body in their spiritual gifts, and develop a passion to reach and impact the world around them.

From *The Next Steps* Class, the believer is invited to make a public confession of faith through water baptism. They are encouraged to invite family and friends, where this can be a celebration of what Christ has done for them.

Lastly, they are invited to attend the Encounter God Retreat.

The next step is **CONNECTING**, where disciple-makers help new believers build relationships with others that will strengthen their relationship with Christ and serve in developing them to one day be disciple-makers themselves.

Chapter 8

Making Disciples: CONNECT

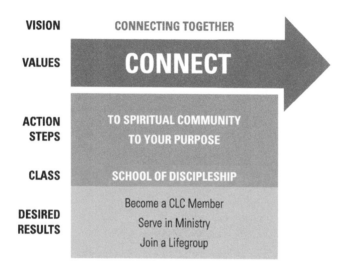

As a new believer continues to build their relationship with God, they also need to learn how to connect to God's family. Up to this point, the new believer has acted like a child, characterized by self-centeredness. The spiritual child needs to know that they belong. The church's role is to take them in as is family. I Tim. 3:15 refers to the church as "God's household ... the pillar and foundation of truth."

A main role of the church is to help Christians discover their gifts and talents. By doing so, the spiritual child can begin the process of understanding their purpose within and through the church.

Connecting with God's Family

As believers grow in this stage, they begin to recognize their need for relationships with other Christians. They have been connected to more mature Christians for the purpose of discipleship, but the focus is all on them. This stage of development calls for them moving beyond themselves to a place of relationship with others.

For many spiritual children, they are disconnected and trying to survive on their own. They show up at church but don't build relationships or realize that connection leads to a bigger purpose. God doesn't want us to go through life on our own. Alton Garrison describes them as orphans who "lack the support and foundation necessary to make it through rough times, and they grow up disassociating with society, feeling burdened by trust issues, and missing out on the power and support of family." 1

From the beginning, the Church was established as the family of God. For spiritual children, it's vital to get them connected to the family so they can be encouraged and continue to grow in their faith. As people share life together, they are united with other brothers and sisters, as well as mothers and fathers in the faith. God gives us one another to help in times of trouble. This creates opportunities for teaching and training that leads to the next stage of spiritual development.

Connecting to Purpose

Connecting to church family not only grows the person individually but also connects the disciple to their purpose in Christ, which can be reflected through the church. They learn more about God's plan to bring all people back into fellowship with Him. As the disciple grows, the disciple-maker can encourage them to use their talents, gifts, and abilities to serve others by getting involved in a ministry both within the church as well as in the community. As they serve, they begin to develop a focus on others and begin to understand how God has a purpose for them to reach others. This begins the next stage of spiritual development—a young adult.

School of Discipleship Class

It's at this point in the transformational process the School of Discipleship Class begins. We typically will begin within a week of the Encounter God Weekend.

As described earlier, SOD will encourage and enable the participant to begin a process of spiritual growth. It's much easier to see Encounter participants sign up for SOD because our experience has been that God has captured their heart with His heart, and the peace and joy they have received is what propels and inspires them to continue in the process. We share on the Encounter that the entire journey continues into SOD. Having received many breakthroughs and an increased passion for the Lord, most want to maintain this victory.

Desired Results

The desired results of the Connect phase is accomplished primarily through SOD. We begin working with the participants to connect with a Life Group before the end of Level One, as it is a prerequisite to Level Two. Our experience is a majority have already gotten connected to a Life Group before they even start SOD, and it was their Life Group Leader who encouraged them to attend the Encounter and SOD.

At the end of SOD Level Two that participants are offered the ability to become a church member. Church attendees can also become a member by attending a Saturday morning class called *DNA Membership*. In this four-hour class, we cover Mission, Vision, Strategy, Fundamental Beliefs and give the participants the ability to join a Life Group and sign up for a ministry. During this time, there is a Q & A session that enables participants to receive all the important information needed to make the decision of becoming a church member.

Individuals are more likely to
attend weekend worship services
when they have a role in ministry.

CLC has a congregational model of church governance; therefore, Church membership is important, as members have the right to elect their deacons and trustees of the church that comprise of the Church Board. The Board approves and presents the annual budget to membership and any constitutional changes to the constitution. The Senior Pastor is the visionary leader of the church, managing pastors and staff to fulfill the church's mission, vision, and strategy. Membership is important for congregants to be a part of the acceptance and approval of important church-related matters.

The final aspect of the Connect phase is joining a ministry. At this phase, we are only encouraging involvement in ministry, for this will increase their passion to serve the Lord and more relationships within the church. Since the pandemic, we also discovered that individuals are more likely to attend weekend worship services when they have a role in ministry. Often individuals are able to self-identify passions and spiritual giftings; we strive to help them learn their SHAPE in the Train phase.

The next step in this process requires **TRAINING** to equip them to serve in the area(s) God has called them, as well as learning the disciple-making process.

Chapter 9

Making Disciples: TRAIN

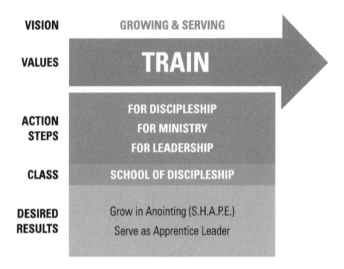

VISION	GROWING & SERVING
VALUES	**TRAIN**
ACTION STEPS	FOR DISCIPLESHIP FOR MINISTRY FOR LEADERSHIP
CLASS	SCHOOL OF DISCIPLESHIP
DESIRED RESULTS	Grow in Anointing (S.H.A.P.E.) Serve as Apprentice Leader

At this step of the process, the disciple is maturing into a spiritual young adult. He or she is beginning to move from self-centeredness to other-centered. This phase of discipleship is characterized by **service**.

For this to take place, the focus needs to be on equipping the next generation of leaders. This starts with the pastor and leaders of the church. A good way to proceed is to build a TEAM. Alton Garrison best describes the acronym of TEAM as: building *trust*, *empowering* team members to make decisions, providing *accountability*, and creating a climate of *mentorship*.

The best way to accomplish this is by enlisting both the disciple and the disciple-maker. If the church leadership can present the vision in such a way that the believers can grasp it, it opens the door for knowledge, behavior, and love to work together and for Christ to be glorified.[1]

The Apostle Paul understood this and explained to the Galatians that the freedom God called them to walk in should be seen as they "serve one another humbly in love. For the entire law is fulfilled in keeping this one command: 'Love your neighbor as yourself." (Gal 5:13-14, NIV).

In this stage, the disciple begins to learn about their gifts and talents, and the disciple-maker continues to walk with them and encourage them while intentionally showing them how to use their gifts to minister to others as they honor God.

In this stage, the disciple begins to learn about their gifts and talents, and the disciple-maker continues to walk with them and encourage them while intentionally showing them how to use their gifts to minister to others as they honor God. As the disciple-maker trains, they can point out the benefits and blessings of serving so that the disciple doesn't look at serving as a burden. This shift in thinking is important because the disciple begins to see the bigger picture of being trained to serve.

The Apostle Paul tells believers, "Don't be selfish; don't try to impress others. Be humble, thinking of others as better than yourselves. Don't look out only for your own interests, but take an interest in others, too" (Phil 2:3-4, NLT).

The intentional leader gives disciples a place to serve and grow as they work through the stage of spiritual young adult. Jesus modeled this with His disciples. Throughout the gospels, we see Jesus providing multiple ways for the disciples to participate in ministry, such as: helping others, preaching publicly, and healing people. Luke 9:1-11 tells how Jesus sent His disciples out to preach the kingdom of God and heal the sick in neighboring villages.

As the disciple walks through this process, they continue to be trained and come to better understand the combination of their giftings, unique personality, and experiences. An intentional leader, with the guidance of the Holy Spirit, can give the disciple an opportunity to serve in ways that can potentially open a door for them to fulfill their purpose.

School of Discipleship Continues

In this phase of Training, we see SOD Level Two and Three helping participants continue in their spiritual journey. In Level Two, we take several weeks helping the participant discover their Spiritual Gifts and how to use them within the CLC context of ministry. This is often referred to as "discovering your anointing." Learning to walk in God's divine design enables them to walk in their anointing. SHAPE is an acrostic representing Spiritual Gifts, Heart/passions, Abilities, Personality, and Experiences. We use several tools and assessments to help them discover their SHAPE.

Desired Results

Levels Two and Three prepare the participants in many of the desired steps as they are trained for ministry, disciple-making, and leadership. Many lessons in SOD deal with leading small groups, as well as growing in the art of leadership. They will learn the mission, vision, and strategy of CLC through SOD. This process is the heart of training at CLC as one is growing and developing.

A new desired result was added recently to this phase, Apprentice Leadership. It was discovered that as participants were finishing SOD, the leap into leadership was too vague and too large of a step for many. As we would try to encourage current leaders to engage these new graduates into leadership roles, it was discovered that this was not happening, mainly due to the lack of experience and/or commitment to the ministry for current leaders to feel confident to turn over responsibilities to the graduate. Having tried many ways to bridge this issue, we finally discovered it would be better to develop a "join me" in leadership step. This allows the new graduate to come alongside leaders and begin to practically learn the aspects of the ministry and develop the confidence and commitment to take on larger levels of responsibility. This step of the development process often leads an apprentice to become an assistant to the leader and eventually a leader in the ministry or group.

A "join me" in leadership step allows the new graduate to come alongside leaders and begin to practically learn the aspects of the ministry and develop the confidence and commitment to take on larger levels of responsibility.

We are often asked, "What is the difference between an apprentice and an assistant?" The simple answer is that an apprentice is learning how to lead in the area of ministry they are serving, whereas an assistant is able to lead when the leader is unable to lead.

We also have added a ministry role to help assist all graduates in getting connected as apprentice leaders. In the final class of SOD, participants are encouraged to become an apprentice in one of three areas: (1) Cadre Group of SOD; (2) Life Group; (3) Department Ministry. We have found that these three areas all undergird the movement of the CLC mission and vision.

When disciples become disciple-makers, they will be released and be able to **RELEASE**, the final phase of the discipleship process.

But it is not a final phase in a linear sense. At the end of the Release phase, the cycle of Share→Connect→ Train→Release begins all over again, as the new disciple-makers begin walking new disciples all the way through the process, and seasoned disciple-makers begin a new round with new believers, resulting in multiplication.

Chapter 10

Making Disciples: RELEASE

In the fourth stage of the CLC Discipleship Process, disciples should now be spiritually mature enough to accept the responsibility to begin the process of intentionally discipling others.

The Apostle John understood this process of moving from childhood in Christ to maturity in the faith:

> "I have written to you who are
>
> God's children
> because you know the Father.

I have written to you who are mature in the faith
because you know Christ, who existed from the
beginning" (1 John 2:14, NLT)

An intentional disciple-maker equips and then releases his or her disciple to become spiritual parents for other disciples, thus multiplying the Kingdom of God. Some may refer to it as reproducing, which is partially true. It's not reproducing a copy of ourselves but reproducing faith in others. Mike Clarensau describes it as having a significant influence on them, so they may act a little bit like us, but their own unique traits and experiences will empower them. In that way, "we don't reproduce ourselves; we make disciples."[1]

Jesus himself told us how to make disciples. In Matthew 28:20, he says, "Teach these new disciples to obey all the commands I have given you" (NLT).

The promise of anointing given to the disciples to go and
make disciples needed to be done
through the power of the Holy Spirit.

Based on Jesus's own words, He wants us to teach others what He taught us. How do we do that? Share our story. Spend time encouraging and sharing life with these new believers. Get them into the Word so that their mind and heart can be renewed. Encourage them to grow in learning and applying these aspects into their lives so that they may continue to develop spiritually. It's not just about head knowledge. Clarensau says, "teach others to crave God's presence and purpose and never forget their ongoing need for God's help and power."[2]

The power of the New Testament Church came from waiting on the Holy Spirit. Jesus told his disciples, "But you will receive power when the Holy Spirit comes upon you. And you will be my witnesses, telling people about me everywhere—in Jerusalem, throughout Judea, in Samaria, and to the ends of the earth" (Acts 1:8, NLT).

This promise of anointing was given to the disciples, that they would go out and make disciples, multiplying the kingdom of God. But it needed to be done through the power of the Holy Spirit. They were told to stay in a room until the Holy Spirit came upon them. Acts 2 begins with the believers being in one place and the Holy Spirit coming and empowering them: "And everyone present was filled with the Holy Spirit and began speaking in other languages, as the Holy Spirit gave them this ability" (Acts 2:4, NLT).

Acts 2:5-41 tells how the crowd outside heard the disciples speaking in different languages, and those visiting the city heard them speak in their native language. The Apostle Peter went out and boldly preached about who Jesus was, why he came to the earth, and all that he did to reconcile people back to God. He spoke a message of true repentance, and many believed and were baptized that day, adding to the church. This was the beginning of the true church and remains the call of the church today.

The Apostle Paul describes the process of reproducing disciples to the Church to his "spiritual son," Timothy:

> "You have heard **me** teach things
> that have been confirmed by many **reliable witnesses**.
> Now teach these truths to other **trustworthy people**
> who will be able to pass them on to **others**"
> (2 Tim 2:2, NLT).

Spiritual parents release their disciples as Messengers of Hope to reproduce disciples who intentionally feed themselves and others from God's Word and rely on the body of Christ to encourage each other to fulfill the mission.

In The Church Life Model, Dr. Lee asks, "Isn't this Christ's expected outcome for His disciples?"[3] He's referring to one going through the process of discipleship and learning to be more like Christ as he/she matures and then producing the fruit of making disciples, which is multiplication in the kingdom of God. As a disciple comes to the stage of being released to reproduce, they continue to encounter God intimately and, as a result, can be a true leader within the church.

School of Ministry

As one finishes SOD, they are encouraged to continue their growth in *School of Ministry*, SOM. Classes are offered three times a year in three specific areas: Bible, Theology, and Practical Ministry. The courses follow the Assemblies of God suggested courses for ministerial training. In fact, CLC uses Global University Berean as the core curriculum. Classes run for ten to twelve weeks, and CLC pastors or outside professors teach the courses. These classes were being offered in-person prior to the pandemic, but since the pandemic have been offered in a virtual format. This has enabled CLC to secure professors from different universities, which has increased the quality and level of teaching, enabling us to glean from experts in their field.

Leaders are encouraged to take one to two classes a year as their schedules allow. We are cautious to not over train and equip the leaders but to inspire them to continue to grow as they serve in ministry. The balance inspires them as they continue to sharpen the edge of their spiritual gifts and growth in the Lord and ministry.

However, we also want to be cautious that they do not only take classes and not engage in ministry. Therefore, we do keep SOM restricted to those that are actively serving in ministry.

One other aspect of ongoing training and equipping is *Leaders Advance*. Several times throughout the year, CLC gathers its leaders together to cast vision and realign in strategy. Often this will include guest speakers or times of spiritual refreshing and renewing. These are considered regional events where all campuses of CLC participate. It's always an encouraging time as leaders see and hear the Big Dream and can sense they are a part of something bigger and larger that is making an impact for the Kingdom of God.

Desired Results

The desired results of the *Release* phase have no specific timeline, as this depends on the leader as they engage in ministry and disciple-making.

If we once again look at the cycler diagram, we can see that the transformational process never ends. As leaders, we, in fact, maybe ministering and working with several who are at different stages of the vision. God continues to add to our "numbers daily those who are being saved" as we continue to lead them in through the transformational process.

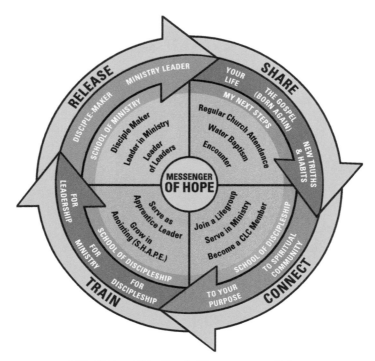

CLC's Global Partnerships

Some of CLC Global partners have chosen to link with CLC in the implementation of SOD. In this case, CLC helps train pastors to be able to teach SOD in their local churches. After attending an Encounter Retreat, the pastor enters into a virtual SOD, where the pastor receives an email weekly with a link to the lessons for that week, discussion questions, and quiz. At their convenience, the pastor watches the lesson and interacts with the discussion board. Every three to four weeks, Pastor Tom holds a live Zoom call with these pastors to help them understand the principles and how to implement them in their local church.

Conclusion

Every organization has a lifecycle. This includes the church. The need for church revitalization, especially in the United States remains: "Struggling churches, disillusioned pastors, and disenchanted believers litter the church landscape. Many of the survivors have no vision for the future! They are simply hanging on by their fingernails hoping for a better day."[1]

But there is hope. The church as an organization may be at a crossroads, and it's up to the leadership to determine if they are willing to honestly assess where they're at in terms of the true health of the church and if they're willing to lead the people, with the help of the Holy Spirit into a season of new life. Through tested principles and a proven process, this book gives pastors a tool they can utilize to walk their church through revitalization.

This process isn't just for churches in America. It's been used in churches around the world. To carry out the mission of Christ, churches around the world need to evaluate where they're at in the lifecycle and be willing to create new lifecycles of growth for a healthy church. It is just as important to carry out God's commandment to multiply as it is planting new churches.

The book, *DiscipleShift*, shares a broad overview of areas to look at as a church works to be healthy and implement ways to fulfill God's purpose to be disciple-makers. They include the following: (1) as a leadership team, develop the biblical vision for your church; (2) as a leadership team, create a common language and definition of terms; (3) develop the process for creating disciples, then give it to those leading the training; (4) consistently live out your vision and consistently recast re-cast your vision; (5) constantly assess, correct and encourage.[2] This will look different for each church, based on your own traditions, programs, and other unique features. This is another tool that can be used to assess the health of the church as it strives to bear the fruit of fulfilling the call that God has given His church.

We must accept the charge and
continue the mission of Christ.

It remains my prayer that the messengers of the Church receive the challenge and exhortation presented in this book. May this challenge be embraced, met with discernment, and received through the empowerment of the Spirit: "Now it's up to you. Be on your toes—both for yourselves and your congregation of sheep. The Holy Spirit has put you in charge of these people—God's people they are—to guard and protect them. God himself thought they were worth dying for" (Acts 20:28, The Message). We must accept the charge and continue the mission of Christ.

105

Endnotes

Introduction

[1] Win Arn, *The Pastor's Manual for Effective Ministry* (Monrovia, CA: Church Growth, 1988), 41.

[2] Aubrey Malphurs and Gordon E. Penfold, *Re:Vision: The Key to Transforming Your Church* (Grand Rapids, MI: Baker Books, 2014), 26.

Chapter 1: The State of the Church

[1] Thom S. Rainer, *Breakout Churches: Discover How to Make the Leap* (Grand Rapids, MI: Zondervan, 2005), 45; Thom S. Rainer, *Autopsy of a Deceased Church* (Nashville: B&H Publishing Group, 2014), 7.

[2] David T. Olson, *The American Church in Crisis: Groundbreaking Research Based on a National Database of over 200,000 Churches* (Grand Rapids, MI: Zondervan, 2008), 179.

[3] David Kinnaman, "Americans Divided on the Importance of Church," Barna Research Group, accessed February 12, 2016, https://www.barna.org/barna-update/culture/661-americans-divided-on-the-importance-of-church#.Vs0p785VVKM.

[4] The American Church Research Project, "The State of the American Church," The American Church, accessed February 22, 2016, http://www.theamericanchurch.org/.

[5] Olson, 35.

[6] General Council of the Assemblies of God, *Index to 2015 AG Statistical Reports*, General Council of the Assemblies of God, accessed July 14, 2016, http://agchurches.org/Sitefiles/Default/RSS/AG.org%20TOP/AG%20Statistical%20Reports/2015%20(year%202014%20reports)/2014%20Full%20Statistical%20Report.pdf

[7] David Kiannman, "10 Facts About America's Churchless," Barna Research Group, accessed February 12, 2016, https://www.barna.org/barna-update/culture/698-10-facts-about-america-s-churchless#.Vs0mR85VVKM.

[8] Aubrey Malphurs and Gordon E. Penfold, *Re:Vision: The Key to Transforming Your Church* (Grand Rapids, MI: Baker Books, 2014), 26.

[9] David Kinnaman, *You Lost Me: Why Young Christians Are Leaving the Church and Rethinking Faith* (Grand Rapids, MI: Baker, 2011), 22.

[10] Ed Stetzer and Mike Dobson, *Comeback Churches: How 300 Churches Turned Around and Yours Can Too* (Nashville: B & H Publishing Group, 2007), 25-26.

[11] Ichak Adizes, *Corporate Lifecycles: How and Why Corporations Grow and Die and What to Do about It* (Paramus, NJ: Prentice Hall, 1988), 202.

[12] Robert D. Dale, *To Dream Again* (Nashville: Broadman Press, 1981), 8.

[13] Martin F. Saarinen, *The Life Cycle of a Congregation* (Bethesda, MD: The Alban Institute, 1986).

[14] George Bullard, "The Life Cycle and Stages of Congregational Development," Evangelical Free Church of America, Southeast District, accessed February 12, 2016, http://sed-efca.org/wp-content/uploads/2008/08/stages_of_church_life_bullard.pdf.

[15] Ibid.

[16] Alton Garrison, *A Spirit-Empowered Church* (Springfield, MO: Influence Resources, 2015), 94.

[17] Ibid.

[18] Ibid.

[19] Ibid.

[20] Ibid.

[21] Gary L. McIntosh, *There's Hope for Your Church: First Steps to Restoring Health and Growth* (Grand Rapids, MI: Baker Books, 2012), 30.

[22] David Moberg, *The Church as a Social Institution: The Sociology of American Religion* (Englewood Cliffs, NJ: Prentice-Hall, 1962), 118-119.

[23] Ibid.

[24] Arnold L. Cook. *Historical Drift: Must My Church Die?* (Camp Hill, PA: Christian Publication, 2000), 12.

Chapter 2: Major Causes for Plateau and Decline

[1] Gary L. McIntosh, *Taking Your Church to the Next Level: What Got You Here Won't Get You There* (Grand Rapids, MI: Baker Books, 2009),16.

[2] George Barna, *Turn-Around Churches* (Ventura, CA: Regal Books, 1993), 33-38.

[3] Stetzer and Dobson, 128-129.

[4] McIntosh, *There's Hope for your Church*, 45.

[5] Malphurs and Penfold, 26.

[6] Reggie McNeal, *Missional Renaissance: Changing the Scorecard for the Church* (San Francisco, CA: Jossey-Bass, 2009), 11.

[7] Malphurs and Penfold, 119.

[8] The re-envisioning curriculum can be found in chapters 9 through 14, the practical application portion of Malphurs's and Penfold's book, *Re:Vision: The Key to Transforming Your Church*.

[9] McNeal, 42.

[10] Olson, 134-135.

[11] Lyle E. Shaller, *Hey, That's Our Church* (Nashville: Abingdon Press, 1975), 39-50.

[12] Ibid.

[13] Malphurs and Penfold, 179.

[14] Ibid., 255-256.

[15] Ibid., 180.

16 Ibid.

Chapter 3: The Process of Transformation

1 Wayne and Sherry Lee, *The Church Life Model: A Biblical Pattern for the Spirit-Filled Church* (Lake Mary, FL: Creation House, 2011), 7.
2 Stetzer and Dobson, 180.
3 Olson, 138.
4 Brain D. McLaren, *The Church on the Other Side: Doing Ministry in the Postmodern Matrix* (Grand Rapids, MI: Zondervan, 2000), 14.
5 Barna, *Turn-around*, 114-115.
6 Malphurs and Penfold, 29.
7 Wayne Lee, "Leadership Development" (class lecture for PTH 900: Issues in Church Life at Assemblies of God Theological Seminary, Springfield, MO, October 25-30, 2010).
8 Ibid.
9 Stetzer and Dobson, 45-50
10 Thom S. Rainer and Eric Geiger, *Simple Church: Returning to God's Process for Making Disciples* (Nashville: B&H Publishing Group, 2006), 139.
11Ibid., 139.
12 Mark Rutland, *Relaunch: How to Stage an Organizational Comeback* (Colorado Springs: David C Cook, 2013), 128.
13 Michael Fletcher, *Overcoming Barriers to Growth* (Minneapolis, MN: Bethany House, 2003), 25-26.
14 Dave Earley, *Turning Members into Leaders: How to Raise Up Your Group Members to Lead New Groups* (Houstons: Cell Group Resources, 2001), 58; George Barna, *Leaders on Leadership* (Ventura, CA: Regal Books, 1997), 48-49.
15 Rutland, 23.
16 Malphurs and Penfold, 31.
17 George Barna, *Turning Vision Into Action* (Eugene, OR: Wipf & Stock Publishers, 1996), 149.
18 John P. Kotter, *Leading Change* (Boston, MA: Harvard Business Review Press, 1996), 9.
19 Rutland, 99.
20 McIntosh, *There's Hope for your Church*, 38.
21 Richard Foster, *Celebration of Discipline* (New York: Harper Collins, 1998), 5.
22 John C. Larue Jr., "Back from the Brink," *Your Church*, September/October 2006, 10.
23 Thom S. Rainer, *The Book of Church Growth: History, Theology, and Principles* (Nashville: B & H Publishers, 1993), 183-84.
24 Cook, *Historical Drift*, 34.
25 Eddie Gibbs, *Church Next: Quantum Changes in How We Do Ministry* (Downers Grove, IL: InterVarsity Press, 2000), 12.
26 Carl George, *Prepare Your Church for the Future* (Grand Rapids, MI: Fleming H. Revell, 1993), 28.

[27] Wayne H. Lee, *Church Life* (Chatom, AL: Church Life Resources, 2004), section 5, 1.

[28] Olson, 137.

[29] Stetzer and Dobson, 15.

[30] Rainer and Geiger, 26.

[31] Randy Frazee, *The Connecting Church: Beyond Small Groups to Authentic Community* (Grand Rapids, MI: Zondervan, 2001), 35.

[32] Lee and Lee, *The Church Life Model: A Biblical Pattern for the Spirit-Filled Church*, 51-52.

[33] Ibid.

[34] Nelson Searcy, *Fusion: Turning First-Time Guests into Fully-Engaged Members of Your Church* (Ventura, CA: Regal, 2007), 27-28.

[35] Ibid.

[36] Randy Frazee, *Making Room for Life* (Grand Rapids, MI: Zondervan, 2003), 33.

[37] George, 85.

[38] Jonathan Gainsbrugh, *Winning the Backdoor War* (Elk Grove, CA: Harvest Church, 1993), 25.

[39] Ibid.

[40] McIntosh, *Taking Your Church to the Next Level*, 166.

[41] Andy Stanley and Bill Willits, *Creating Community: 5 Keys to Building a Small Group Culture* (Colorado Springs: Multnomah Books, 2004), 45.

[42] Stetzer and Dobson, 152.

[43] Rainer and Geiger, 62.

[44] Ibid., 63.

[45] Ibid., 68.

[46] Stanley and Willits, 72.

[47] Rainer and Geiger, 142.

[48] Ibid., 155.

[49] Ibid., 142.

[50] Ibid., 158-159.

[51] Ibid., 158.

[52] Stetzer and Dobson, 127.

[53] John Palmer, *Equipping for Ministry* (Springfield, MO: Gospel Publishing House, 1990), 16.

[54] Lee, Section 10, 4.

[55] Christian C. Schwarz, *Natural Church Development: A Guide to Eight Essential Qualities of Healthy Churches* (St. Charles, IL: ChurchSmart Resources, 2003), 22-23.

[56] Schwarz, 24.

[57] Lee, Section 10, 3.

[58] Stetzer and Dobson, 132.

[59] Joel Comiskey, *Leadership Explosion* (Houston: Touch Publications, 2000), 16.

[60] Robert James Clinton, *Spiritual Gifts* (Alberta, Canada: Horizon House, 1985), 37, 125.

[61] McIntosh, *There's Hope for your Church*, 63.

[62] McNeal, 6-7.

[63] Stetzer and Dobson, 6.

[64] Wayne Lee, Section 12, 5.

[65] McNeal, 55.

[66] Mike Erre, *Death by Church* (Eugene, OR: Harvest House Publishers, 2009), 137.

[67] Ibid., 124.

[68] McNeal, 126.

[69] Ibid.

[70] Rutland, 73.

[71] Rainer and Geiger, 72.

[72] Ibid.

[73] Aubrey Malphurs, *Advanced Strategic Planning: A New Model for Church and Ministry Leaders* (Grand Rapids, MI: Baker Books, 1999), 11.

[74] Malphurs and Penfold, 168.

[75] Samuel R. Chand, *Cracking Your Church's Culture Code: Seven Keys to Unleashing Vision & Inspiration* (San Francisco: Jossey-Bass, 2011), 9-16.

[76] Ibid.

[77] Rutland, 60.

[78] Lee, Section 13, 2.

[79] Stetzer and Dobson, 71.

[80] Kenneth L. Callahan, *Twelve Keys to an Effective Church* (San Francisco: Harper Collins, 1983), 163.

[81] Lee, 71.

Chapter 4: Creating New Lifecycles

[1] McIntosh, *Taking Your Church to the Next Level*, 90-95.

[2] Ibid., 99.

[3] Ibid.

[4] Ibid.

[5] Ibid, 197.

[6] Stetzer and Dobson, 27.

[7] Andy Stanley, *Deep & Wide: Creating Churches Unchurched People Love to Attend* (Grand Rapids, MI: Zondervan, 2012), 302-306, Kindle.

[8] Michael A. Beitler, *Strategic Organizational Change: A Practitioner's Guide for Managers and Consultants*, 3rd ed. (Greensboro, NC: Practitioner Press International, 2013), 39.

[9] Kotter, 22.

[10] Malphurs and Penfold, 207.

[11] Ibid.

[12] Erwin Raphael McManus, *An Unstoppable Force: Daring to Become the Church God Had in Mind* (Orange, CA: Group Publishing, 2001), 23.

[13] Kotter, 37.

[14] Ibid.

[15] Kotter, 58.

[16] Alton Garrison, *A Spirit-Empowered Church*, 92.

[17] Ibid., 211.

[18] Kotter, 22.

[19] Rutland, 153.
[20] Kotter, 125, 127.
[21] Ibid., 154.
[22] Beitler, 48.
[23] Kotter, 165.
[24] McIntosh, *Taking Your Church to the Next Level*, 198.
[25] Ibid.
[26] McIntosh, *There's Hope for Your Church*, 52-53.

Chapter 5: The Process of Creating a New Lifecycle

[1] Lee, section 6, page 1.
[2] Ibid.
[3] Peter Wagner, *Church Planting for a Greater Harvest* (Ventura, CA: Regal, 1990), 67-70.
[4] Lee, Section11, page 1.

Chapter 6: The Process of Making Disciples: An Introduction

[1] Mike Clarensau, *A Spirit-Empowered Life* (Springfield, MO: Vital Resources, 2015), 161.

Chapter 9: Making Disciples: Train

[1] Ibid., 185.

Chapter 10: Making Disciples: Release

[1] Clarensau, *Spirit-Empowered Life*, 137.
[2] Ibid., 138.
[3] Wayne and Sherry Lee, *The Church Life Model* (Lake Mary, FL: Creation House, 2011), 62.

Conclusion

[1] Aubrey Malphurs and Gordon E. Penfold, *Re:Vision: The Key to Transforming Your Church* (Grand Rapids, MI: Baker Books, 2014), 22.
[2] Jim Putman and Bobby Harrington with Robert E. Coleman, *DiscipleShift: Five Steps That Help Your Church to Make Disciples Who Make Disciples* (Grand Rapids, MI: Zondervan, 2013), 230.

Printed in the USA
CPSIA information can be obtained
at www.ICGtesting.com
LVHW061120120923
757853LV00010B/651